Powerpoint for Windows® 95
Made Simple

Powerpoint for Windows® 95 Made Simple

Moira Stephen

MADE SIMPLE
BOOKS

Made Simple
An imprint of Butterworth-Heinemann
Linacre House, Jordan Hill, Oxford OX2 8DP
A division of Reed Educational and Professional Publishing Ltd

℞   A member of the Reed Elsevier plc group

OXFORD BOSTON JOHANNESBURG
MELBOURNE NEW DELHI SINGAPORE

First published 1996
Reprinted 1997
© Moira Stephen 1996

TRADEMARKS/REGISTERED TRADEMARKS
Computer hardware and software brand names mentioned in this book are protected
by their respective trademarks and are acknowledged.

British Library Cataloguing in Publication Data
A catalogue record for this book is available from the British Library

ISBN 7506 2817 0

Typeset by P.K.McBride, Southampton

Archtype, Bash Casual, Cotswold and Gravity fonts from Advanced Graphics Ltd
Icons designed by Sarah Ward © 1994
Printed and bound in Great Britain by Scotprint, Musselburgh, Scotland

Contents

Preface IX

1   Getting Started   1

What is PowerPoint?.. 2
Getting into PowerPoint 3
PowerPoint dialog box 4
PowerPoint window.. 5
PowerPoint objects 6
Summary 8

2   Help   9

Contents tab 10
Index tab 13
Find tab 14
Answer Wizard 16
And yet more Help... 17
Summary 18

3   The new Presentation   19

AutoContent wizard..20
Template 24
Blank Presentation..26
Starting within PowerPoint 28
Saving a presentation 29
Closing down 30
Opening a presentation 31
Summary 32

4   Basic techniques   33

AutoContent Wizard Slides 34
Moving between slides 35
Replacing sample text 36
Adding text items 37
Demote and promote 38
Paragraph spacing 39
Adding new slides 40
Entering and editing text 41
Summary 42

5   Enhancing slides   43

Formatting your text 44
Bullets 47
Changing a slide layout 48
Slide notes 49
Changing the template 51
Background styles 52
Re-arranging your slides 54
Deleting slides 55
Headers & footers 56
Summary 58

6   Outline View   59

Setting up the outline 60
Entering text 61
New slides 62
Promoting & demoting 64
Collapse the outline 65
Rearranging an outline 66
Deleting slides 67
Summary 68

7	Drawing	69

Selecting objects 70
Text tool 72
Drawing tools 73
Free rotate tool 74
AutoShapes 75
Fill, line and shadow 76
Drawing+ toolbar 78
Manipulating objects 79
Summary 82

8	Graphs	83

Starting a graph 84
Datasheet and toolbars 86
Chart type 88
Customising graphs 89
Colours and patterns 91
Leaving the graph 93
Summary 94

9	More objects...	95

Organisation charts 96
Text and boxes 98
Text and drawing tools 100
Zoom options 102
Finishing touches 103
Update and exit 104
Tables 105
The ClipArt gallery 107
Choosing a picture 108
Media clips 110
Summary 114

10   Masters   115

Slide master 116
Title master 118
Handout master 119
Notes master 121
Summary 122

11   Slide Shows   123

Slide sorter view 124
Hide slide 125
Transitions 126
Build 128
Rehearse Timings 130
Slide Show 132
Slide Show options 135
Summary 136

12   Printing Presentations   137

Slide format 138
Printing slides 140
Printing notes pages 142
Printing handouts 143
Printing outline view 145
Summary 146
Index 147

Index   143

Preface

The computer is about as simple as a spacecraft, and who ever let an untrained spaceman loose? You pick up a manual that weighs more than your birth-weight, open it and find that its written in computerspeak. You see messages on the screen that look like code and the thing even makes noises. No wonder that you feel it's your lucky day if everything goes right. What do you do if everything goes wrong? Give up.

Training helps. Being able to type helps. Experience helps. This book helps, by providing training and assisting with experience. It can't help you if you always manage to hit the wrong keys, but it can tell you which are the right ones and what to do when you hit the wrong ones. After some time, even the dreaded manual will start to make sense, just because you know what the writers are wittering on about.

Computing is not black magic. You don't need luck or charms, just a bit of understanding. The problem is that the programs that are used nowadays look simple but aren't. Most of them are crammed with features you don't need – but how do you know what you don't need? This book shows you what is essential and guides you through it. You will know how to make an action work and why. The less essential bits can wait – and once you start to use a program with confidence you can tackle these bits for yourself.

The writers of this series have all been through it. We know your time is valuable, and you don't want to waste it. You don't buy books on computer subjects to read jokes or be told that you are a dummy. You want to find what you need and be shown how to achieve it. Here, at last, you can.

1 Getting Started

What is PowerPoint? 2

Getting into PowerPoint 3

PowerPoint dialog box 4

PowerPoint window 5

PowerPoint objects 6

Summary 8

What is PowerPoint?

PowerPoint for Windows 95 is a presentation graphics package. If you have to make presentations, PowerPoint gives you the tools you need to produce your own materials with little or no help from presentation graphics specialists.

You can use PowerPoint to produce:-

Slides

Slides are the individual pages of your presentation. They may contain text, graphs, clip art, tables, drawings, animation, video clips, visuals created in other applications, shapes – and more!! PowerPoint will allow you to run your slide show on your computer, or as 35mm slides or overhead projector transparencies.

Speaker's Notes (Sections 4, 5, 10 & 12)

A Speaker's Notes page accompanies each slide you create. Each notes page contains a small image of the slide plus any notes you type in. You can print the pages and use them to prompt you during your presentation.

Handouts (Sections 10 & 12)

Handouts consist of smaller, printed versions of your slides which can be printed 2, 3 or 6 slides to a page. They provide useful backup material for your audience and can be customised with your company name or logo.

Outline (Sections 6, 10 & 12)

A presentation Outline contains the slide titles and main text items, but neither art nor text typed in using the text tool. The Outline gives a useful overview of your presentation's structure.

Take note

A PowerPoint presentation is a collections of slides, with (optional, but useful) support materials, notes, handouts and your outline, all in one file.

Getting into PowerPoint

Is PowerPoint installed on your computer? If it isn't, install it now (or get someone else to do it for you).

If necessary, switch on your computer and go into Windows. You are now ready to start.

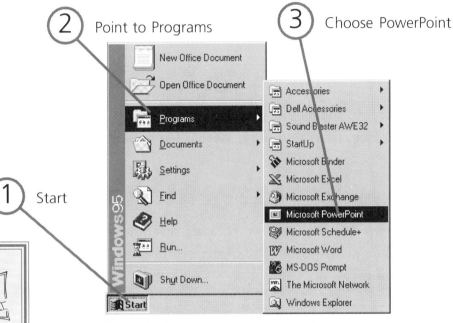

(2) Point to Programs

(3) Choose PowerPoint

(1) Start

The Tip of the Day appears each time you go into PowerPoint. Tips can be useful learning aids when you are getting to know the package.

Deselect to switch off the Tip of the Day

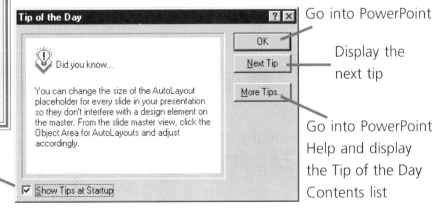

Go into PowerPoint

Display the next tip

Go into PowerPoint Help and display the Tip of the Day Contents list

PowerPoint dialog box

After the Tip of the Day, you arrive at the PowerPoint dialog box, where you start to set up your presentation.

AutoContent Wizard

Choose this if you want to start by using a Wizard that helps you work out the content and organisation of your presentation.

Template

This option lets you pick a presentation template with the colour scheme, fonts and other design features already set up.

Blank Presentation

If you opt for this one, you get a blank presentation with all the colour scheme, font and design features set to the default values.

Tip

If you need to know more about Windows 95, try the companion volume in this series – Windows 95 Made Simple.

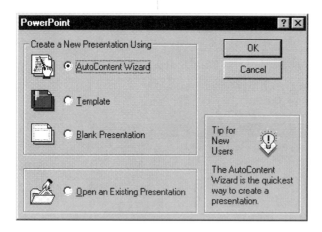

Open an Existing Presentation

This option takes you to the Open dialog box, where you can open an existing presentation.

PowerPoint window

The PowerPoint window is very similar to other Microsoft application windows. If you use Word, Excel or Access you will recognise some of the tools on the Toolbars.

The Standard and Formatting Toolbars usually appear along the top of the window. The Drawing Toolbar is usually down the left hand side of the window.

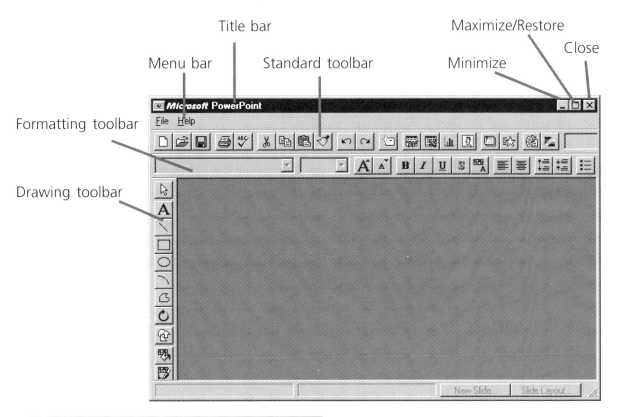

Title bar

Maximize/Restore

Close

Menu bar

Standard toolbar

Minimize

Formatting toolbar

Drawing toolbar

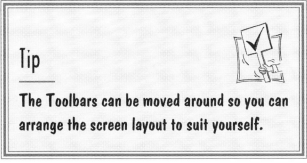

Tip

The Toolbars can be moved around so you can arrange the screen layout to suit yourself.

PowerPoint objects

When working in PowerPoint you work with *objects*. The objects may be:-

- Text
- Drawings
- Graphs
- Organisation Charts
- Clip art
- Tables

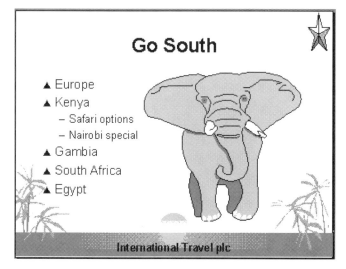

Clip art can enliven your text – a wide variety of images are supplied with PowerPoint

Annotated graphs can be produced very easily

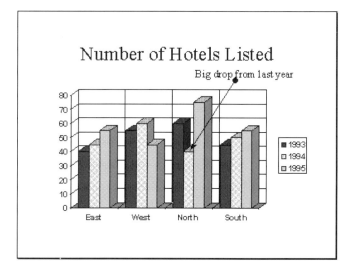

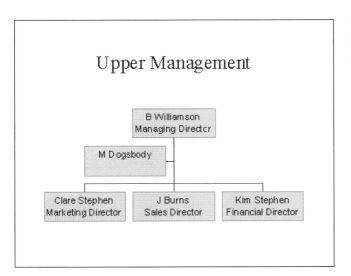

Organisation charts are simple to create – once you've worked out the structure of your organisation!

Word tables are useful for displaying statistics

Take note

You'll learn how to create and manipulate these objects as you work with the package.

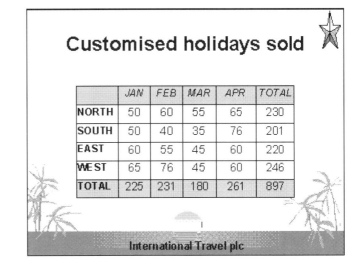

Customised holidays sold

	JAN	FEB	MAR	APR	TOTAL
NORTH	50	60	55	65	230
SOUTH	50	40	35	76	201
EAST	60	55	45	60	220
WEST	65	76	45	60	246
TOTAL	225	231	180	261	897

International Travel plc

Summary

- ❑ PowerPoint is a powerful presentation graphics package

- ❑ The Tip of the Day displays a feature or shortcut you may find useful when using PowerPoint

- ❑ The PowerPoint dialog box gives you a range of options to get you started creating your presentation

- ❑ The PowerPoint window displays a selection of toolbars to give you quick access to commonly used features in the package

- ❑ Text, Drawings, Graphs, Organisation Charts, Clip art and Tables are called PowerPoint Objects

2 Help

Contents tab .10

Index tab 13

Find tab 14

Answer Wizard 16

And yet more Help... 17

Summary .18

Contents tab

When working in the Windows environment there is always plenty of help available – in books, in manuals, in magazines and on-line. The trick is being able to find the help you need, when you need it. In this section, we look at the various ways you can interrogate the on-line Help when you discover you're in need of it.

The usual way into Help is through the Help Menu. We'll consider the PowerPoint Help Topics first. From the Help Topics dialog box, you can interrogate the Help system from the

● Contents tab

● Index tab

● Find tab or

● Answer Wizard tab

We'll consider the Contents tab first. The Contents tab is a handy place to "browse" from to find out what's in the Help system.

1. Open the Help menu
2. Choose Help Topics
3. At the Help Topics dialog box, select the Contents tab
4. Select a "book" that interests you
5. Click Open to open the book
6. Choose a topic from the book
7. Click Display
8. Point to a "hot spot" that interests you and click on it
9. Click Help Topics to return to the Help Topics dialog box

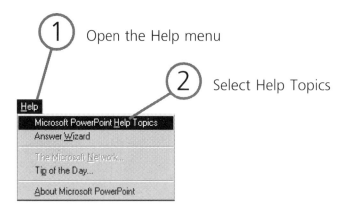

1 Open the Help menu

2 Select Help Topics

Help
Microsoft PowerPoint Help Topics
Answer Wizard
The Microsoft Network...
Tip of the Day...
About Microsoft PowerPoint

Tip

If you've used previous versions of PowerPoint, take a look through the What's New pages in the on-line help.

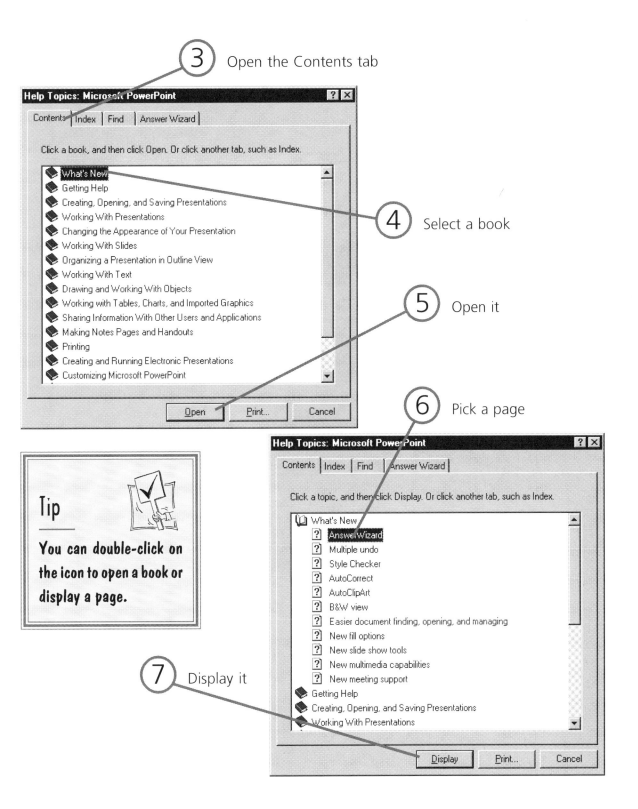

③ Open the Contents tab

Help Topics: Microsoft PowerPoint

Contents | Index | Find | Answer Wizard

Click a book, and then click Open. Or click another tab, such as Index.

- What's New
- Getting Help
- Creating, Opening, and Saving Presentations
- Working With Presentations
- Changing the Appearance of Your Presentation
- Working With Slides
- Organizing a Presentation in Outline View
- Working With Text
- Drawing and Working With Objects
- Working with Tables, Charts, and Imported Graphics
- Sharing Information With Other Users and Applications
- Making Notes Pages and Handouts
- Printing
- Creating and Running Electronic Presentations
- Customizing Microsoft PowerPoint

Open | Print... | Cancel

④ Select a book

⑤ Open it

⑥ Pick a page

Tip

You can double-click on the icon to open a book or display a page.

Help Topics: Microsoft PowerPoint

Contents | Index | Find | Answer Wizard

Click a topic, and then click Display. Or click another tab, such as Index.

- What's New
  - Answer Wizard
  - Multiple undo
  - Style Checker
  - AutoCorrect
  - AutoClipArt
  - B&W view
  - Easier document finding, opening, and managing
  - New fill options
  - New slide show tools
  - New multimedia capabilities
  - New meeting support
- Getting Help
- Creating, Opening, and Saving Presentations
- Working With Presentations

Display | Print... | Cancel

⑦ Display it

To get help while you're working, click Answer Wizard on the Help menu.

The new Answer Wizard uses IntelliSense™ technology to determine the type of help you need. When you type a request in your own words on the Answer Wizard tab, the wizard will supply answers that will help you get your work done.

You can also find assistance on the Contents tab or the Index tab. To look for specific words or phrases, click the Find tab.

Close if you have finished

(8) Click on a "hot spot" to open its panel

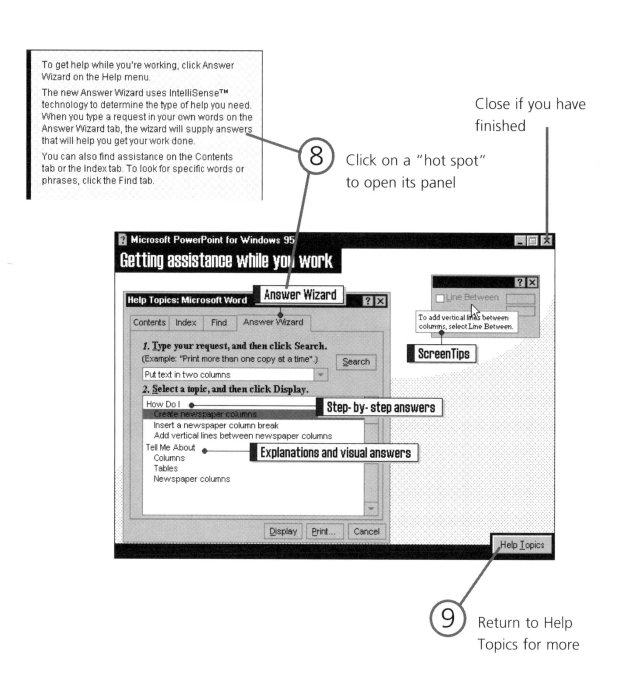

(9) Return to Help Topics for more

12

Basic steps

1 Open the Help menu and choose Help Topics

2 At the Help Topics dialog box, select the Index tab

3 Start typing the word you're looking for

4 Select an index entry from the list

5 Click Display

6 Select one from the Topics Found list

7 Click Display

8 Close the Help window when you have finished

Index tab

The Index tab gives you quick access to any topic and is particularly useful once you know what you are looking for!

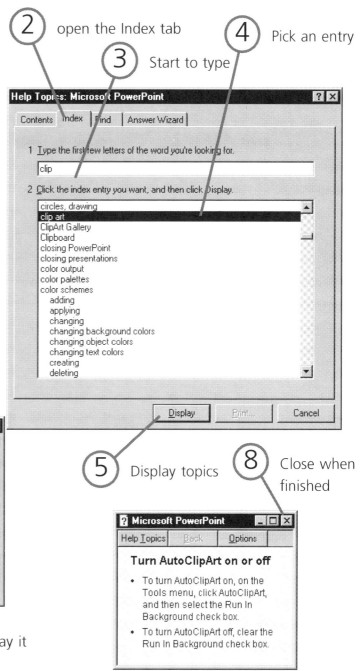

② open the Index tab   ④ Pick an entry

③ Start to type

⑤ Display topics   ⑧ Close when finished

⑥ Pick a topic

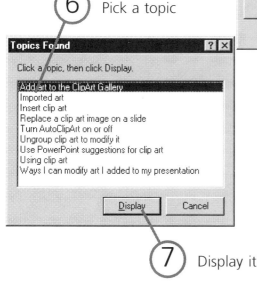

⑦ Display it

Find tab

You can use the Find tab to search out specific words and phrases, rather than look for a particular category of information.

If this is the first time you've used the Find tab the Find Setup Wizard runs to set up your word list – just follow the prompts to set up your list (this only happens once).

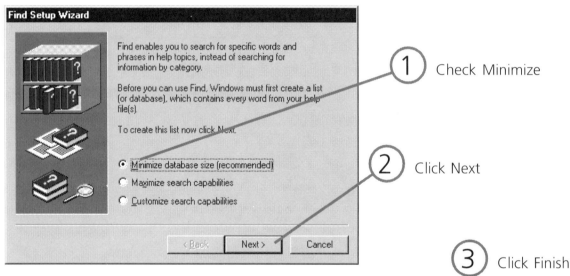

Check Minimize

Click Next

Click Finish

Minimize database size gives you only the most relevant help pages

Maximize indexes almost everything on every help page – overkill!

Customize is best left to the experts

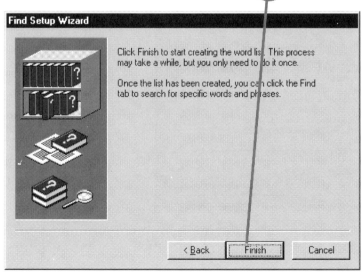

Basic steps

1 Select the Find tab
2 Type in your word – or enough of it to get some matching words displayed
3 Select a matching word to narrow the search
4 Choose a topic
5 Click Display
6 Close the Help when you are done

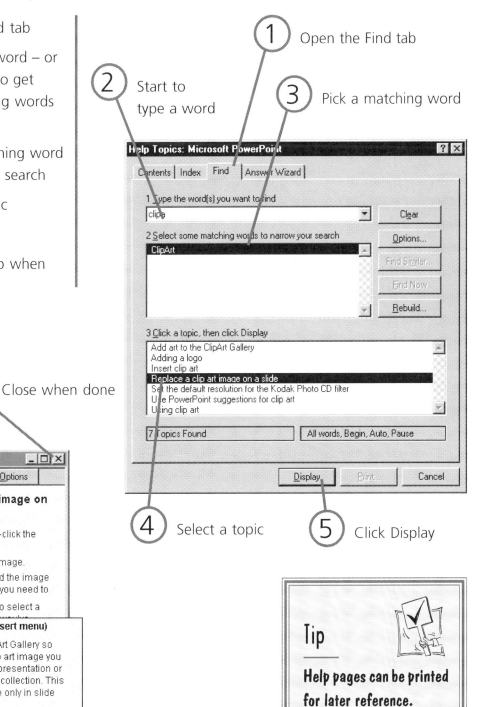

(1) Open the Find tab

(2) Start to type a word

(3) Pick a matching word

Help Topics: Microsoft PowerPoint ? ✕

Contents | Index | Find | Answer Wizard

1 Type the word(s) you want to find

clip ▼ Clear

2 Select some matching words to narrow your search

ClipArt

Options...

Find Similar...

Find Now

Rebuild...

3 Click a topic, then click Display

Add art to the ClipArt Gallery
Adding a logo
Insert clip art
Replace a clip art image on a slide
Set the default resolution for the Kodak Photo CD filter
Use PowerPoint suggestions for clip art
Using clip art

7 Topics Found | All words, Begin, Auto, Pause

Display Print... Cancel

(4) Select a topic (5) Click Display

(6) Close when done

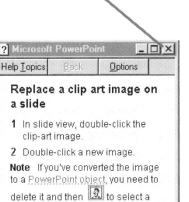

? Microsoft PowerPoint _ ☐ ✕

Help Topics | Back | Options

Replace a clip art image on a slide

1 In slide view, double-click the clip-art image.

2 Double-click a new image.

Note If you've converted the image to a PowerPoint object, you need to delete it and then 🔲 to select a

Clip Art command (Insert menu)

Takes you to the ClipArt Gallery so you can select the clip art image you want to insert in your presentation or to update your clip art collection. This command is available only in slide and notes views.

Tip

Help pages can be printed for later reference.

15

Answer Wizard

Using the Answer Wizard, you can interrogate the Help system by asking it questions in English. The phrasing of the questions improves with practice, but things like "How do I create a new slide?" or "How do I animate an object?" do work.

1 Select Answer Wizard from the Help menu or open the tab

2 Type in your question

3 Click Search

4 Choose a topic from the list

5 Click Display

6 Work through the Answer Wizard as it demonstrates the procedure

7 Click anywhere outside the display to close

① Go to Answer Wizard

② Ask your question

③ Click Search

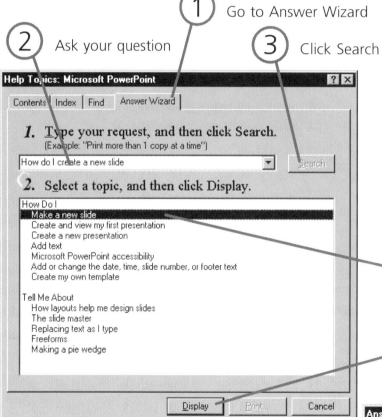

④ Pick a topic

⑤ DIsplay it

⑦ Click anywhere to close

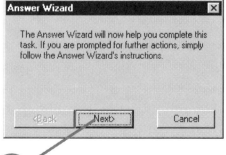

⑥ Step through the Wizard

16

Basic steps

1 Click ![Help] the Help tool on the Standard toolbar

2 Point and click on the tool or menu item you are interested in

❑ A prompt appears to describe the function of the tool or menu item

And yet more Help...

Help Tool

You can get help on any tool on a displayed toolbar, or on any menu item, using the Help tool.

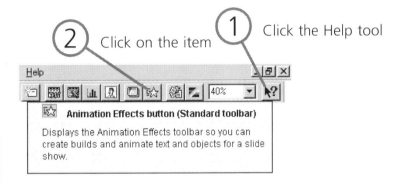

② Click on the item   ① Click the Help tool

Tooltips

If you point to any tool on a displayed toolbar, a tooltip appears to describe the function of the tool. The status bar displays a short description of the tool's function.

Rest the pointer on the tool for a moment to see the tip ...

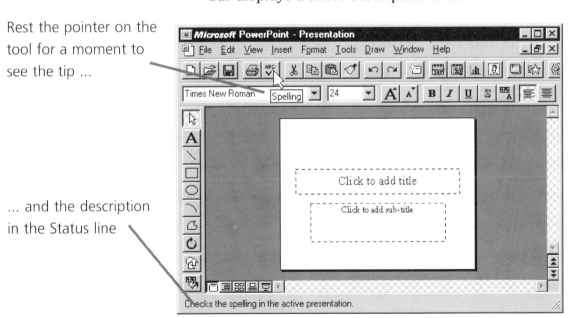

... and the description in the Status line

Summary

❑ To access PowerPoint Help system, select Microsoft PowerPoint Help Topics from the Help menu

❑ Browse through the Help from the Contents tab

❑ Search for specific categories of information from the Index tab

❑ Locate help on specific words using the Find tab

❑ Ask questions of the Help system using the Answer Wizard

❑ Tooltips and the Help tool are useful learning aids when you start out using PowerPoint

3 The new Presentation

AutoContent wizard 20

Template 24

Blank Presentation 26

Starting within PowerPoint 28

Saving a presentation 29

Closing down 30

Opening a presentation 31

Summary 32

AutoContent wizard

Basic steps

1 Start up PowerPoint and go to the PowerPoint dialog box

2 Select the AutoContent Wizard

3 Click [OK]

4 The first dialog box simply tells you what the Wizard does – click [Next >]

In this section we will look at the different options for creating a presentation – we will consider its content later. Whichever option you select, you still end up creating slides, notes and handouts for your presentation.

Once you are into PowerPoint and have closed the Tip of the Day, the PowerPoint dialog box appears.

The easiest way to create your first presentation is to use the AutoContent Wizard. The wizard helps you set up the Title Slide (the first slide in your presentation), and gives you an outline to follow as you build up the other slides.

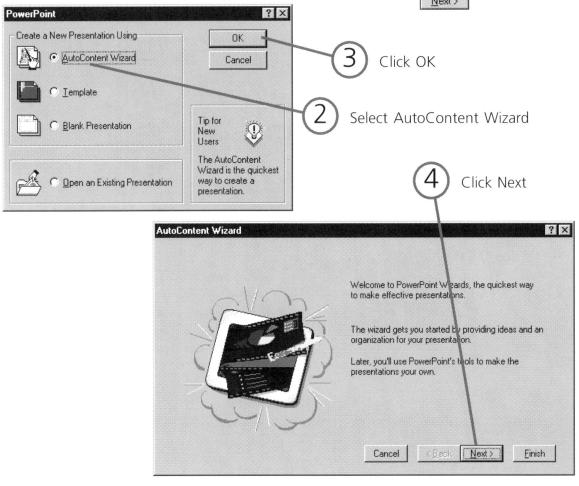

③ Click OK

② Select AutoContent Wizard

④ Click Next

20

5 Provide any information you wish to appear on the Title slide and click Next >

6 Select the option that best describes the type of presentation you are going to give and click Next >

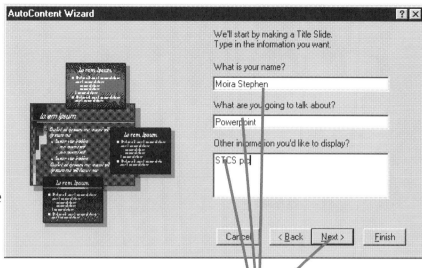

5 Supply Title slide details and click Next

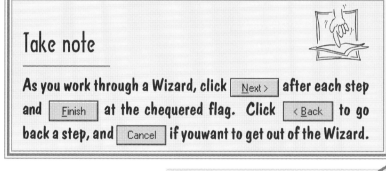

6 Set the option and click Next

The layouts and styles are designed to suit the type of message being delivered

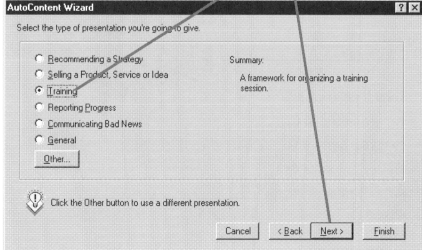

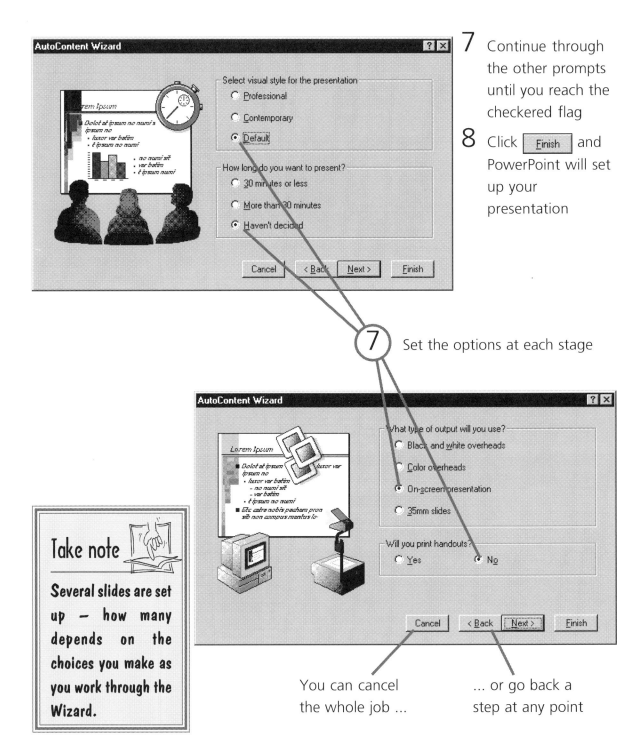

7 Continue through the other prompts until you reach the checkered flag

8 Click [Finish] and PowerPoint will set up your presentation

⑦ Set the options at each stage

Take note

Several slides are set up – how many depends on the choices you make as you work through the Wizard.

You can cancel the whole job ...

... or go back a step at any point

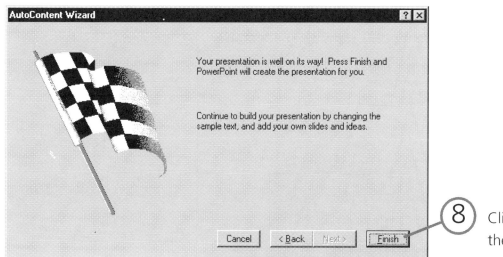

8 Click Finish at the flag

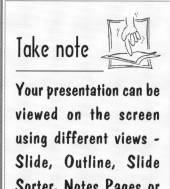

Take note

Your presentation can be viewed on the screen using different views - Slide, Outline, Slide Sorter, Notes Pages or Slide Show. You'll soon learn which view is most appropriate to the task you are doing.

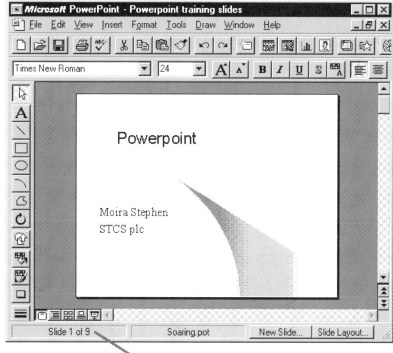

Number of slides created

23

Template

This option lets you start out by choosing the template on which you wish to base your presentation. The template will determine the design elements of your presentation, including font and colour scheme.

Basic steps

1 At the PowerPoint dialog box select the Template option

2 Click [OK]

3 Choose the Presentation design you wish to use from the New Presentation dialog box

4 Click [OK]

❑ If you select from the Presentations tab, you are taken directly to the title slide of your presentation. Stop here!

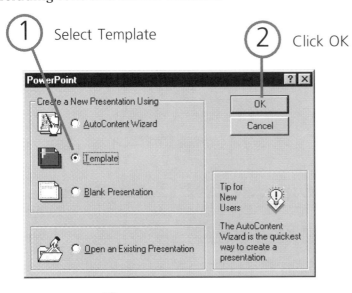

① Select Template   ② Click OK

③ Choose a design

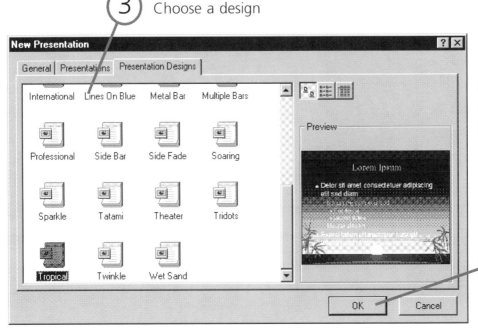

A preview of the selected design is displayed here

④ Click OK

❑ If you select from the Presentation Designs tab, you have not finished yet.

5 At the New Slide dialog box choose a layout for the first slide.

6 Click [OK]

❑ Once PowerPoint has set up the presentation, it displays it in Slide View. The first slide is displayed, ready for your input.

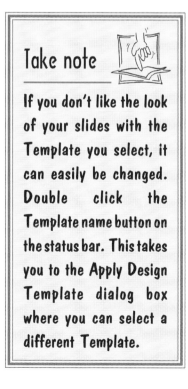

Take note

If you don't like the look of your slides with the Template you select, it can easily be changed. Double click the Template name button on the status bar. This takes you to the Apply Design Template dialog box where you can select a different Template.

⑤ Pick a layout   ⑥ Click OK

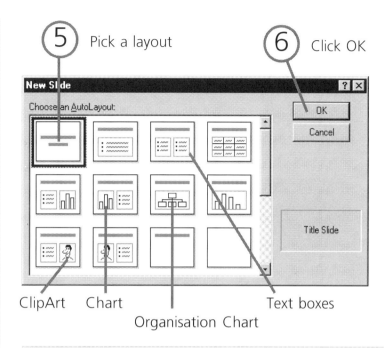

ClipArt   Chart   Text boxes
          Organisation Chart

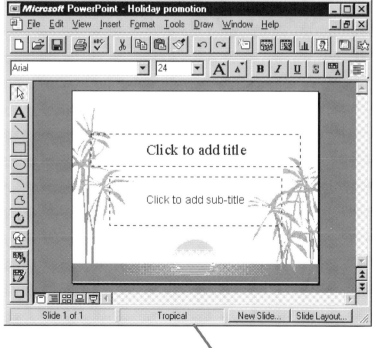

Current Template double-click here to change

25

Blank Presentation

If you prefer to set up your own presentation try the Blank Presentation. The colour scheme, fonts and other design features are set to the default values when you choose this option.

Basic steps

1 At the PowerPoint dialog box select the Blank Presentation option

2 Click [OK]

3 Choose a slide layout for your first slide – usually the Title Slide

4 Click [OK]

❑ Once PowerPoint has set up the presentation, it displays it in Slide View. The slide you chose at step 3 is displayed, ready for your input.

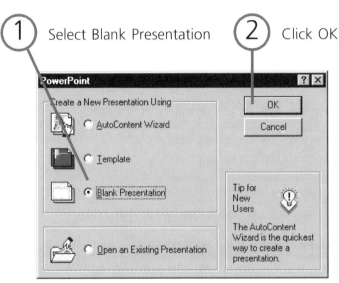

① Select Blank Presentation
② Click OK

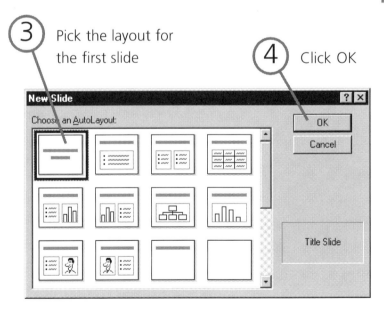

③ Pick the layout for the first slide
④ Click OK

Take note

Some of the slide layouts in the New Slide dialog box have graphic, table, organisation chart and clipart objects set up on them. We will look at these later in the book.

Tip

If you don't like the structured approach of the AutoContent wizard, you may find the "clean" look created by the Blank Presentation option easiest to work with in the early stages of setting up your presentation. The colours, templates and patterns can all be applied later.

Slide ready for completion

Double click here to add a design template later, if wanted.

Take note

You can easily apply a design template later. Double click the Template name button on the status bar. This takes you to the Apply Design Template dialog box where you can select a different Template.

Starting within PowerPoint

The PowerPoint dialog box is not the only place you can create a new presentation from. When working in PowerPoint you can easily create a new presentation at any time.

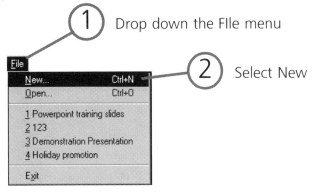

(1) Drop down the FIle menu

(2) Select New

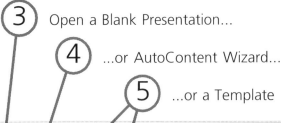

(3) Open a Blank Presentation...

(4) ...or AutoContent Wizard...

(5) ...or a Template

1 Open the File menu

2 Choose New

❑ The New Presentation dialog box opens.

3 To start with a Blank Presentation, select its icon on the General tab

4 To start with AutoContent Wizard, select its icon from the Presentations tab

5 To open a Template, select one either from the Presentations or the Presentation Designs tabs

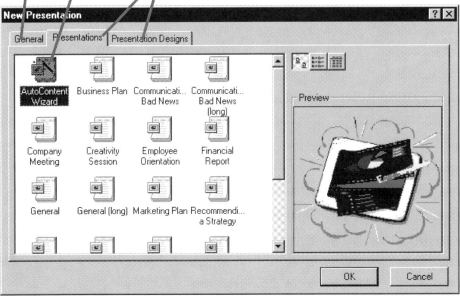

Saving a presentation

1 Click 🖫 the Save tool on the Standard toolbar

2 Specify the Drive and/ or Folder into which you wish to save your presentation

3 Give your presentation a Filename

4 If the presentation is to be viewed on a system that does not have your fonts, click Embed True Type. The fonts are then saved in the presentation file.

5 Click ⌷ Save ⌷

Once you have set up your presentation, you must save it if you want to keep it (if you don't save it, it will be lost when you switch off your computer).

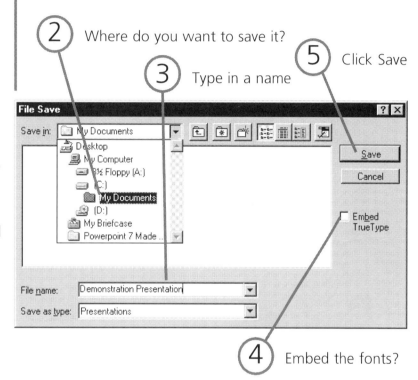

② Where do you want to save it?

③ Type in a name

⑤ Click Save

④ Embed the fonts?

Save Vs Save As

The first time you save a presentation, you are taken to the File Save dialog box to give it a name and specify the folder and drive you want it saved in. Thereafter, any time you save the presentation using the Save tool on the toolbar, the old version of the file is replaced by the new, edited version. This is what you would usually want to happen.

However, if you have saved your presentation, gone on to edit it, then wish to save the edited version using a different filename, or in a different location, open the File menu and choose Save As to get to the File Save dialog box.

Closing down

When you've finished working on your presentation you must save it (see above) and close it.

Leaving PowerPoint is very easy. If you use other Windows packages, the technique is very similar.

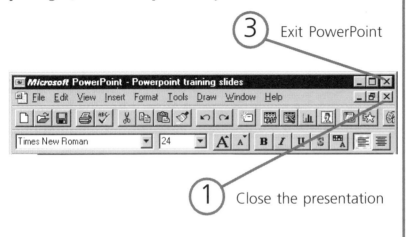

③ Exit PowerPoint

① Close the presentation

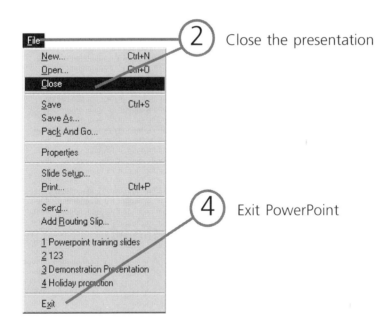

② Close the presentation

④ Exit PowerPoint

❑ Closing a presentation

1 Click the Close button on the Presentation title bar

or

2 Open the File Menu and choose Close

❑ Leaving PowerPoint

3 Click the Close button on the PowerPoint title bar

or

4 Open the File Menu and choose Exit

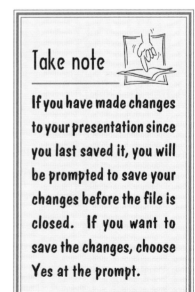

Take note

If you have made changes to your presentation since you last saved it, you will be prompted to save your changes before the file is closed. If you want to save the changes, choose Yes at the prompt.

Opening a presentation

1 Click 🖼 the Open tool
on the Standard
toolbar

or

Open the File menu
and choose Open

2 Select the Drive and
Folder that contains
your presentation file

3 Select the presentation

4 Click [Open]

If you want to work on a presentation you've already
created, saved and closed, you must open it first.

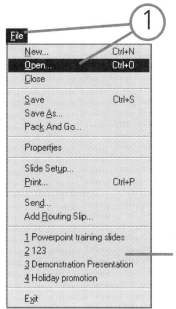

Use File – Open

Take note

**There's an Open Existing
Presentation option on the
PowerPoint dialog box.**

The last 4 presentations
worked on are listed here.
Click the name to open one.

Set the Drive and Folder   Select the file   Click Open

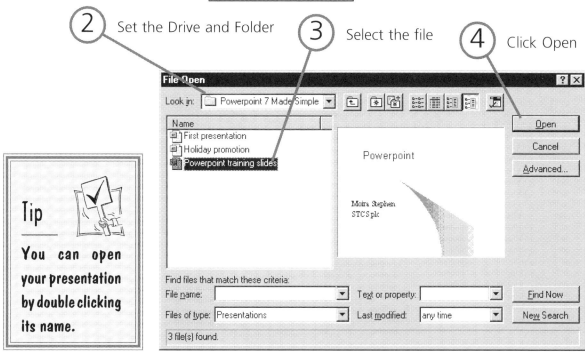

Tip

You can open
your presentation
by double clicking
its name.

Summary

- ❑ When creating a new presentation, you can choose your starting point – the AutoContent Wizard, a Template or a Blank Presentation

- ❑ The easiest/quickest option for your first presentation is probably the AutoContent Wizard

- ❑ The first slide of your presentation is displayed once you have specified your options

- ❑ Regardless of the options selected when you create your presentation, you can easily change any option as your presentation develops

- ❑ Use the Save tool on the Standard Toolbar to save your presentation

- ❑ Click the Close button on the presentation title bar to close the file

- ❑ To Exit PowerPoint, click the Close button on the top title bar

- ❑ Use the file name list in the File menu to open a recently used presentation

- ❑ To create a new presentation from within PowerPoint, choose New from the File menu

4 Basic techniques

AutoContent Wizard Slides 34

Moving between slides 35

Replacing sample text 36

Adding text items 37

Demote and promote 38

Paragraph spacing 39

Adding new slides 40

Entering and editing text 41

Summary 42

AutoContent Wizard Slides

When you create a presentation using the AutoContent Wizard, a *set* of slides is created ready for completion. The number of slides created will vary depending on the options you specified when creating your presentation.

The TITLE SLIDE is displayed in Slide View, complete with the details you provided during the creation stage.

Completing the slides is simply a case of replacing the "sample" text on each of the other slides with what you actually want to say.

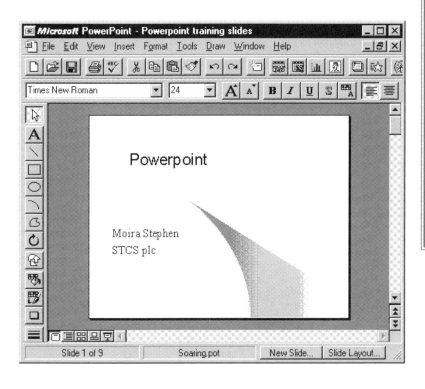

Take note

If you create a presentation using a Presentation Design template a set of slides is also created. The sample text on all slides (including the Title slide) must be replaced with what you want to say.

Moving between slides

1 Drag the elevator up or down the scroll bar to the desired slide.

2 Note the slide number and presentation name that appears when you drag the elevator. Release the mouse button, when you reach the desired slide.

or

3 Click the Previous Slide button to move up

4 Click the Next Slide button to move down

In Slide View, you see one slide at a time on your screen. When you have several slides, you must move up or down through them to view them.

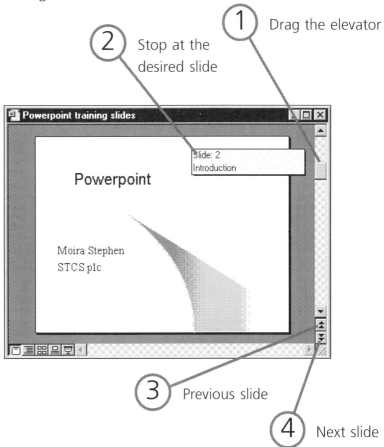

① Drag the elevator

② Stop at the desired slide

③ Previous slide

④ Next slide

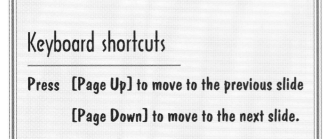

Keyboard shortcuts

Press [Page Up] to move to the previous slide

[Page Down] to move to the next slide.

35

Replacing sample text

When working on a presentation created using either the AutoContent wizard or a Presentation Design template, you must replace the "sample" text with the text you actually want to appear on your slides.

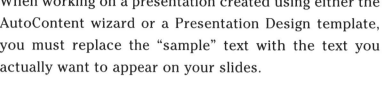

① Click into an area to highlight it

② Select the text

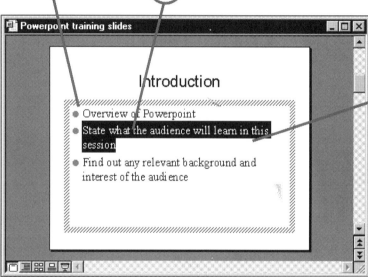

③ Key in new text

Selection techniques

- Click and drag

- Click at one end of the text, move the I-beam to the other end, hold down [Shift] and click the left button

- Single click over the bullet, to the left of the item – (note the 4-arrowed pointer)

- To de-select your text, click anywhere, or move the I-beam using the arrow keys

Adding text items

1 Place the insertion point (the I-beam) at the end of the item you wish to add a new item under

2 Press [Enter]

3 A new bullet appears – just key in your text

If you need more items than are provided in the sample list on any slide, you can easily add more.

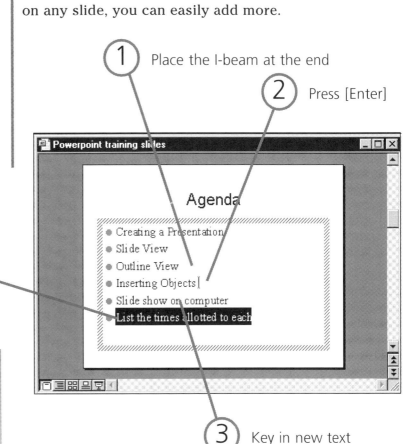

1 Place the I-beam at the end

2 Press [Enter]

Old text selected, ready for deletion

3 Key in new text

Take note

To delete an item from your list, select the item then press [Delete]

Keyboard shortcuts

To **MOVE** an item within your list, select the item then press

[Shift]-[Alt]- [↑] to move the item up through the list

[Shift]-[Alt]- [↓] to move the item down through the list

Demote and promote

Not all items on a slide need to be at the same level. You can structure the points on your slides to show main points and sub-points by demoting (indent further to the right/down a level) and promoting (moving left/up a level) as required.

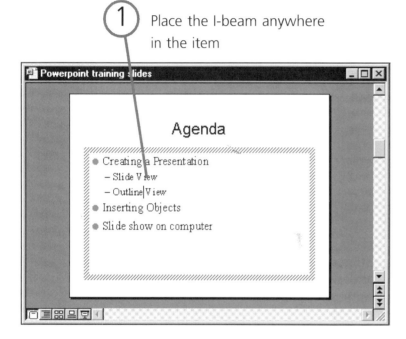

(1) Place the I-beam anywhere in the item

Basic steps

❑ To demote an item

1 Place the insertion point within the item you wish to demote

2 Click ➡ the Demote tool on the toolbar

❑ To promote an item

1 Place the insertion point within the item you wish to promote

2 Click ⬅ the Promote tool on the toolbar

Keyboard Shortcuts

[Shift]-[Alt]- [→] demotes an item

[Shift]-[Alt]- [←] promotes an item

Paragraph spacing

1 Select the paragraphs you wish to increase or decrease the spacing between

2 Click the increase spacing 🔢 or 🔢 decrease spacing tool until you think your slide looks okay

3 De-select the paragraphs

Depending on the number of points you wish to make on a slide, the layout of the slide may look better if you either increase or decrease the amount of space between the paragraphs.

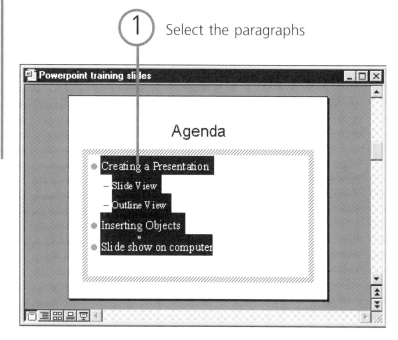

① Select the paragraphs

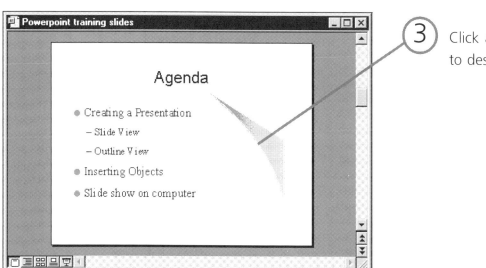

③ Click anywhere to deselect

Adding new slides

As your presentation develops you may need to add more slides to it. You can add them at any place in your presentation. It doesn't matter how you created your presentation – using the AutoContent wizard, a template or a blank presentation – new slides can easily be added as required.

1 View the slide that will be above your new one

2 Click the `New Slide...` button on the Status bar

or

Click the Insert New Slide tool

3 Select the slide layout required from the New Slide dialog box

4 Click `OK`

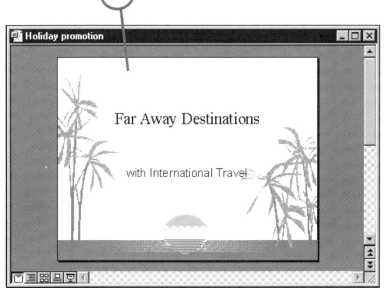

① Go to the slide above the new one

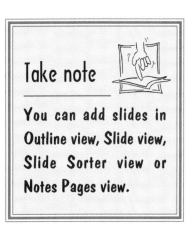

Take note

You can add slides in Outline view, Slide view, Slide Sorter view or Notes Pages view.

③ Select a layout

④ Click OK

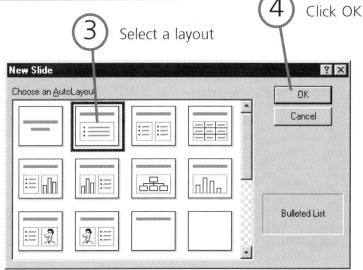

Entering and editing text

Basic steps

❑ Adding text

1 Click in the Title area

2 Key in your text

3 Click in the bulleted list area

4 Key in your text and press [Enter] after each item

5 Repeat step 4 until all your points are listed

❑ Editing text

1 Click to place the insertion point inside the text to be edited

2 Insert or delete characters as required

To enter text into a slide you have just added, simply follow the instructions on the slide!

To edit text on an existing slide, you must first locate the slide you wish to edit, then make the changes required. To edit the text, use the normal Windows techniques.

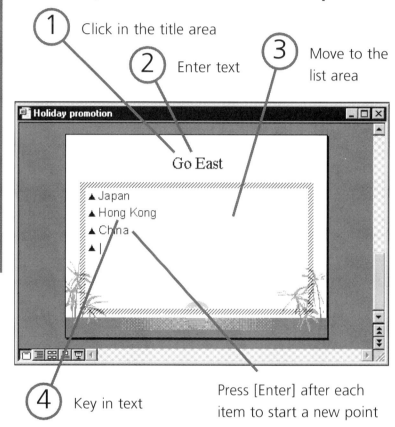

① Click in the title area
② Enter text
③ Move to the list area
④ Key in text

Press [Enter] after each item to start a new point

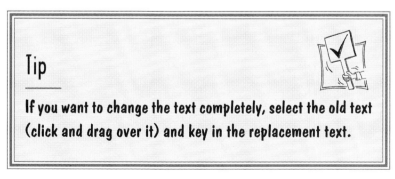

Tip

If you want to change the text completely, select the old text (click and drag over it) and key in the replacement text.

41

Summary

❏ In Slide View you move from slide to slide using the Previous/Next slide buttons, the elevator or [PageUp] and [PageDown]

❏ When working with slides created by the AutoContent Wizard or a Presentation Design template, you must replace the sample text with your own.

❏ To add more items to a slide, simply press [Enter] at the end of the last item

❏ You can structure your slides using the Demote and Promote tools or keyboard shortcuts.

❏ Fine tune the spacing between your paragraphs using the increase spacing and decrease spacing tools

❏ New slides can be added anywhere in your presentation using the New Slide button

5 Enhancing slides

Formatting your text 44

Bullets 47

Changing a slide layout 48

Slide notes 49

Changing the template 51

Background styles 52

Re-arranging your slides 54

Deleting slides 55

Headers & footers 56

Summary 58

Formatting your text

So far, we've accepted the font formats attributed to our text by PowerPoint. You can of course change these at any time using the formatting toolbar.

② Pick a font

③ Set the size

④ Toggle styles on or off

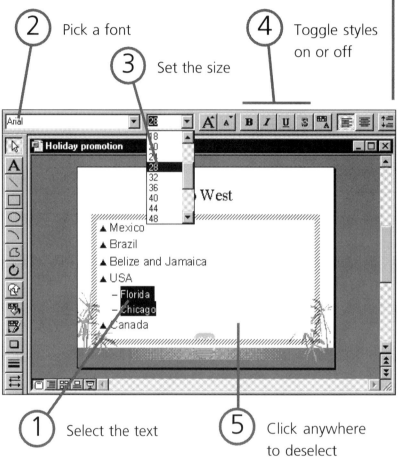

① Select the text

⑤ Click anywhere to deselect

Basic steps

❑ To change the font name, size or style

1 Select the text you want to format

2 Drop down the font list and choose one

or

3 Drop down the font size and choose one

or

4 Click the Bold, Italic, Underline or Shadow tools to switch the format on and off

5 Deselect the text

Tip

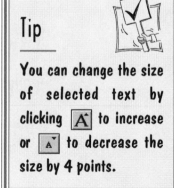

You can change the size of selected text by clicking Ⓐⁱ to increase or Ⓐᵢ to decrease the size by 4 points.

Keyboard shortcuts

[Ctrl]-[B] Bold, [Ctrl]-[I] Italics, [Ctrl]-[U] Underline

These all toggle the style on and off

Basic steps

❏ To change the colour

1 Select the text

2 Click 📷 the Text Color tool to display the range available

3 Click on a colour (or on Other Color... if you want a larger choice)

4 Deselect the text

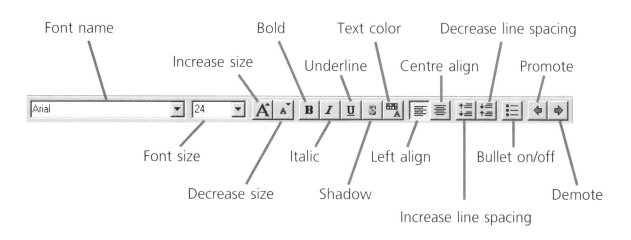

② Click Text Color

① Select the text

③ Pick a colour

Times New Roman · 44 · A˘ A˘ B I U S 📷 ▤ ▤ ▤

Automatic

Other Color...

⚫ Holiday promotion

Go West

▲ Mexico
▲ Brazil
▲ Belize and Jamaica
▲ USA
– Florida
– Chicago
▲ Canada

④ Click anywhere

The Standard toolbar

Font name

Increase size

Bold

Underline

Text color

Centre align

Decrease line spacing

Promote

Arial · 24 · A˘ A˘ B I U S 📷 ▤ ▤ ▤ ▤ ▤ ◆ ◆

Font size

Decrease size

Italic

Shadow

Left align

Bullet on/off

Increase line spacing

Demote

Alignment

In presentations, text is usally aligned to the left or centre. There are tools for both of these. If you do want text to be right aligned or justified (making the text meet both left and right margins), there are options on the Format – Alignment menu.

❑ To justify text

1 Select the text you want to format

2 Click the Left Alignment or Center Alignment tools

4 If you have selected multiple paragraphs or several characters, deselect the text

① Select the paragraph

② Set the alignment

③ Deselect if necessary

Take note

A paragraph is selected if the insertion point is within it, or at least part of it is highlighted – you don't need to select all the characters.

Keyboard shortcuts

[Ctrl]-[L] Left Align
[Ctrl]-[R] Right Align
[Ctrl]-[J] Justify
[Ctrl]-[E] Centre

Basic steps

□ Choosing a bullet

1 Select the point(s)

2 Open the Format menu and choose Bullet

3 Choose a character set

4 Select the character you want to use

5 Set the colour and size

6 Click the [Preview] button to see the effect of your changes on the slide (you might need to move the Bullet dialog box so you can see your slide)

7 Click [OK] to apply your changes to the slide

In most slide layouts the text objects are formatted to display bullets at each point. The bullets can be switched off (and on again) by clicking ⊞. If you do not like the bullets set by PowerPoint, you can choose your own.

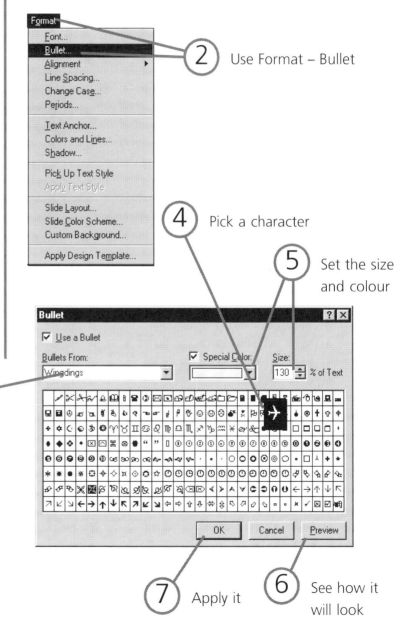

② Use Format – Bullet

④ Pick a character

⑤ Set the size and colour

③ Choose a character set

⑦ Apply it

⑥ See how it will look

Tip

Wingdings, Symbol and Zapf Dingbats have the best bullet characters.

47

Changing a slide layout

If you decide you have chosen the wrong layout for a slide, it is easily changed from Slide view.

We look at inserting clip art in Section 9

1 View the slide whose layout you wish to change

2 Click the [Slide Layout...] button on the Status bar

3 Select the Layout you want to use

4 Click [Apply]

Take note

We look at inserting clip art in Section 9

① View the slide

② Click Slide Layout

④ Click Apply

③ Pick a new layout

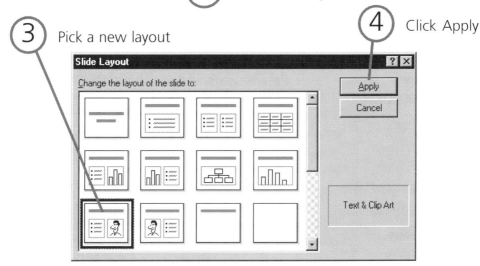

Basic steps

1 Locate the slide you want to make notes for

2 Click 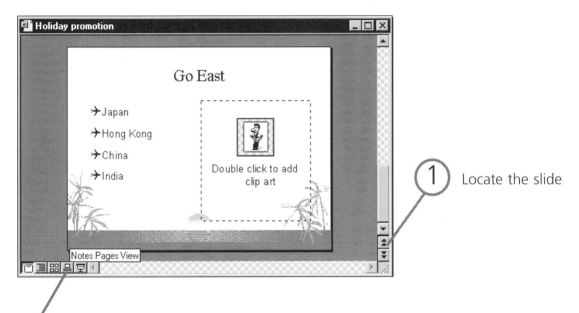 to go into Notes Pages View

cont...

To help you through your presentation, you'll find things a lot easier if you have some notes to accompany your slides. You can add notes in Notes Pages view. The notes pages consist of a copy of the slide plus the notes you type in yourself. The notes pages can be printed out so you can refer to them as you do your presentation (see section 12).

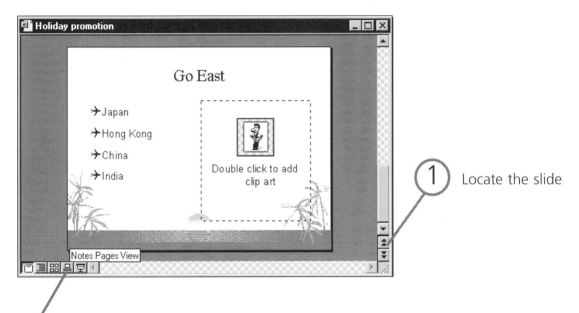

1 Locate the slide

2 Click Notes Pages view

Take note

Your notes are saved automatically when you save your presentation.

Alternative Views

You can work on your presentation in different "Views". You can easily change from one view to another using the view icons at the bottom left of the screen.

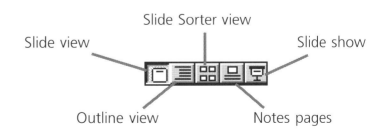

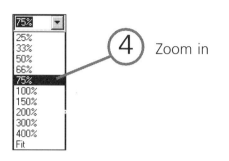

4 Zoom in

3 Click into the Notes area

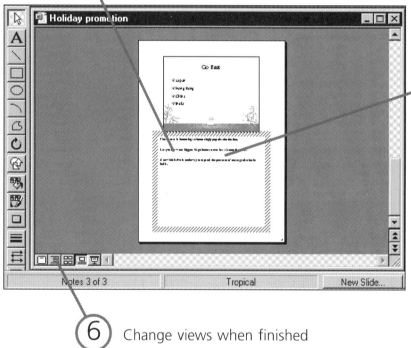

5 Type in notes

6 Change views when finished

Tip

You can stay in **Notes Pages** view and work through all your slides, adding notes as necessary.

Changing the template

1. Double click the Template name field

   [Tropical] on the Status bar

or

2 Click 🔲 the Apply Design Template tool

3 Change the folder if necessary

4 Select the Template you want to use

5 Click [Apply]

You can change your presentation template at any time. The template determines the design elements of your presentation - colour, fonts, alignment of text etc.

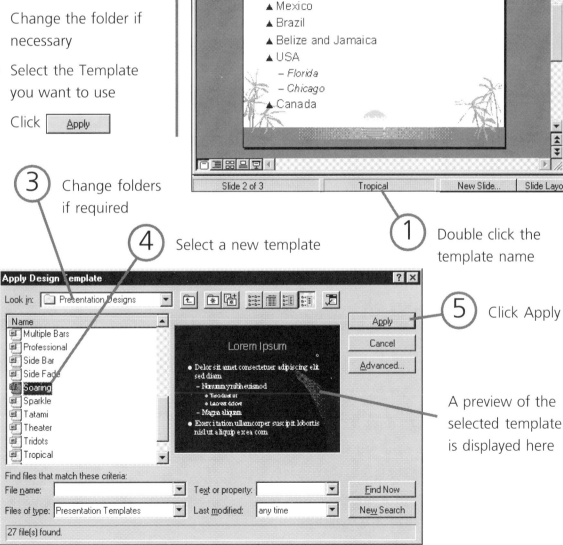

③ Change folders if required

④ Select a new template

① Double click the template name

⑤ Click Apply

A preview of the selected template is displayed here

Background styles

When you select a template for your presentation, the slide background colour and shading is picked up from the options set in the template. You can easily change the colour and shading options while still retaining the other design elements of the template.

If your presentation were in sections, eg on individual departments, or regional figures, you could set a different background colour for each section of your presentation.

1 Open the Format menu

2 Choose Custom Background...

3 Choose a Background Fill option from the list

4 Click [Apply] to apply it to the selected slide only

or

[Preview] to see the effect

[Apply to All] to apply it to all slides

[Cancel] if you don't like the effect

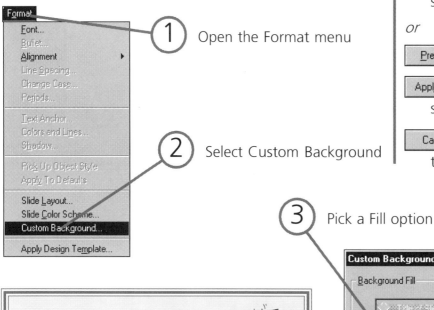

Open the Format menu

Select Custom Background

Pick a Fill option

Apply it

Take note

You can select several slides at once in **Slide Sorter view** (next page). Click the first slide, then hold [Shift] down while you click each of the others. You can then change the background colour of the selected set. If you select the wrong slide, [Shift] click the slide to de-select it.

And yet more options.....

Experiment with the various dialog boxes to see what effects are available

Specify your own shading (1 or 2 colour)

Or choose from the Preset Colours

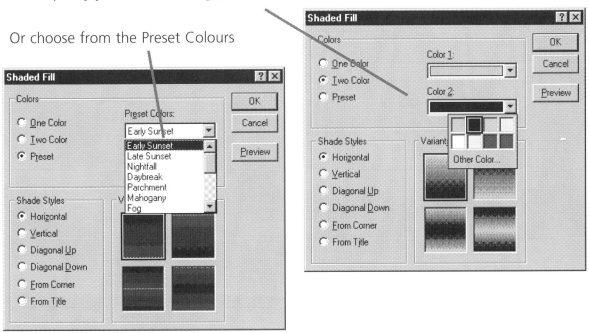

Select a Pattern Fill design and colour scheme

Or try one or the Textured fills

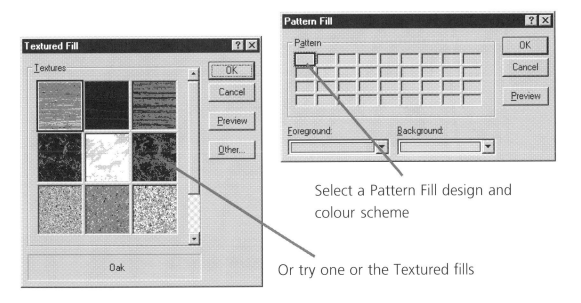

Re-arranging your slides

If you need to re-arrange the order your slides are in, go into Slide Sorter view.

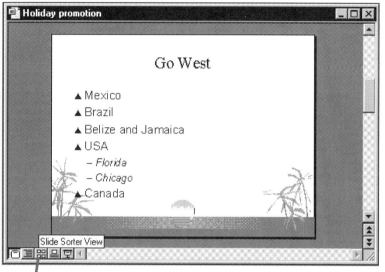

Click Slide Sorter view

1 Click ▦ the Slide Sorter view tool to go into Slide Sorter view

2 Click on the slide you want to move

3 Drag and drop the selected slide into its new position – the dimmed dotted vertical line indicates where it will go.

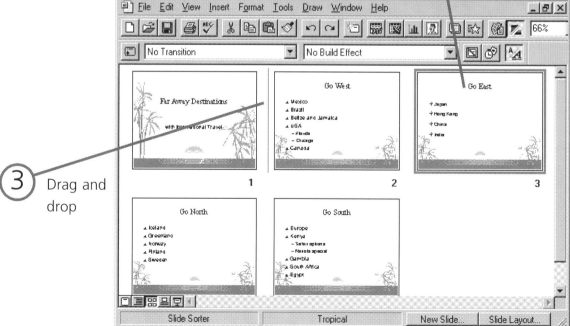

Select the slide

Drag and drop

Basic steps

1 In Slide view, move to the slide you want to delete

2 In Slide Sorter view and Outline view, select the slide you wish to delete

3 Open the Edit menu

4 Choose Delete Slide

As you presentation develops you may decide that you need to delete a slide.

③ Open the Edit menu

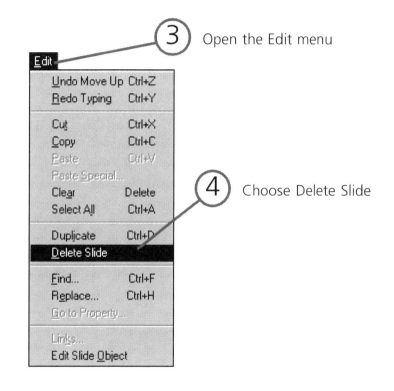

④ Choose Delete Slide

Take note

You can delete slides in Outline view, Slide view, Slide Sorter view or Notes Pages view.

Tip

If you delete a slide by mistake, click the Undo tool on the standard toolbar, or use the keyboard shortcut — [Ctrl]-[Z].

Headers & footers

If you want to add slide numbers, the date, time or any other standard text at the top or bottom of slides, notes or handouts, use the Header and Footer command.

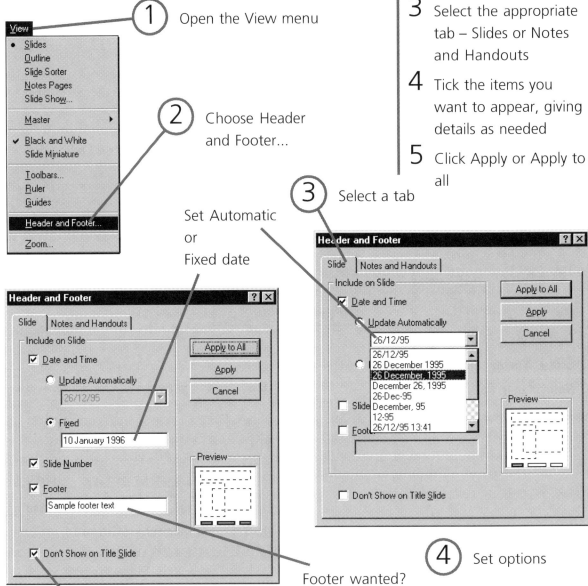

Open the View menu

Choose Header and Footer...

Select a tab

Set Automatic or Fixed date

Footer wanted?

Set options

Select to leave items off title slide

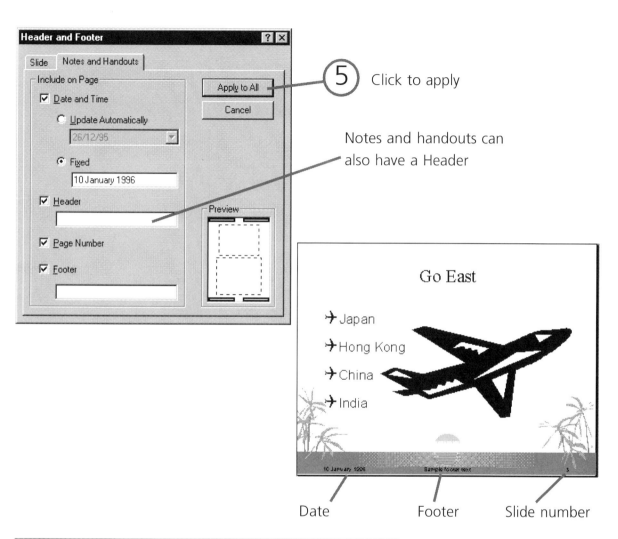

⑤ Click to apply

Notes and handouts can also have a Header

Date   Footer   Slide number

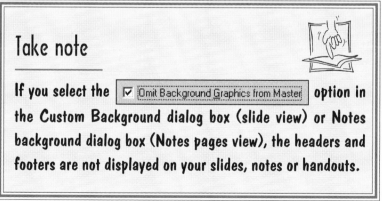

Take note

If you select the [✓ Omit Background Graphics from Master] option in the Custom Background dialog box (slide view) or Notes background dialog box (Notes pages view), the headers and footers are not displayed on your slides, notes or handouts.

Summary

- ❏ You can delete a slide by choosing Delete Slide from the Edit menu

- ❏ To change the layout of a slide, click the Slide Layout button on the status bar then choose the layout you want from the dialog box

- ❏ To change the presentation Template, double click the Template name field on the status bar, then select an alternative Template from the list

- ❏ Go into Slide Sorter view to re-arrange your slides. Then simply click and drag your slides to their new positions

- ❏ You can add notes to your slides in Notes Pages view

- ❏ Headers and footers can be switched on and off from the Header and Footer dialog box

6 Outline View

Setting up the outline 60

Entering text .61

New slides 62

Promoting & demoting 64

Collapse the outline 65

Rearranging an outline 66

Deleting slides 67

Summary 68

Setting up the outline

As an alternative to entering the text onto your slides in Slide view, you might like to try Outline view. In Outline view you can work on your text without the distraction of colour, graphics etc.

You can easily move between Slide view and Outline view using the view tools at the bottom left of the screen.

To change to Outline view, click the Outline view tool.

As well as deciding on the text, you can also determine the structure of each slide (main points, sub-points etc). Your discussion points can be structured into 5 levels if necessary.

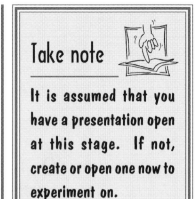

Take note

It is assumed that you have a presentation open at this stage. If not, create or open one now to experiment on.

    Slide Title

   Level 1

      Level 2

         Level 3

            Level 4

               Level 5

The Outlining Toolbar

The Outlining Toolbar is displayed down the left hand side of the screen.

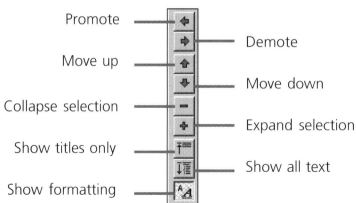

Entering text

1 Position the insertion
   point or select the text
   you want to replace

2 Key in you own text

3 Should you wish to
   make a list of points,
   simply press [Enter]
   after each point to
   move onto a new line

Take note

**Clipart, graphs, drawings
and organisation charts
cannot be added to your
slide in Outline view —
only in Slide view.**

Entering and editing text is done in much the same way as
in Slide view. Either type new text in directly through the
keyboard or , if you wish to replace existing text, simply
select it and key in your replacement text.

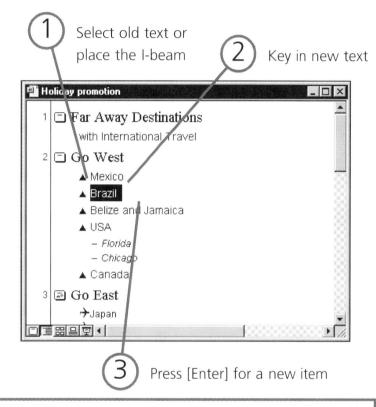

① Select old text or
   place the I-beam

② Key in new text

③ Press [Enter] for a new item

Selecting in Outline view

You can use the same selection techniques as employed in Slide view, or:

To select a point
Single click on the bullet to the left of the point to be selected (note the special
4-headed mouse pointer) or double click to the right of the point to be selected

To select a whole slide
Single click on the slide icon to the left of the slide to be selected

New slides

You can easily add new slides in Outline view. A new slide created in Outline view always has the Bulleted List layout.

Entering text in Outline view is similar to in Slide view.

Basic steps

- ❑ Title Slide Layout
- **1** Key in the Slide Title
- **2** Press [Enter] – a new slide is created
- **3** Click ➡ the Demote tool to move in a level

  With a Title Slide layout, you are taken to the sub-title level text with no bullet
- **4** Key in your sub-title
- **5** Press [Enter]

  You are positioned below the sub-title line, at the same level
- **6** Click ⬅ the Promote tool to move back to slide title level for your next slide

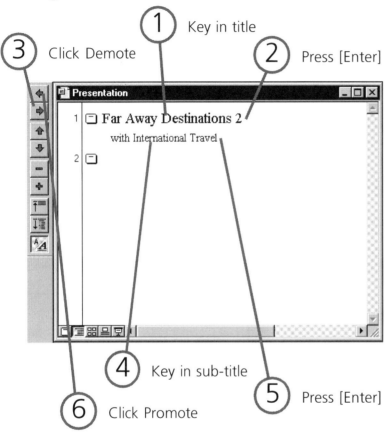

Key in title
Press [Enter]
Click Demote
Key in sub-title
Press [Enter]
Click Promote

Take note

If you press [Enter] at the end of an existing slide, a new bulleted list layout slide is inserted.

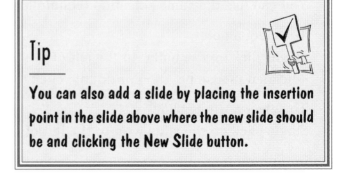

Tip

You can also add a slide by placing the insertion point in the slide above where the new slide should be and clicking the New Slide button.

Basic steps

❑ Bulleted List Layout

1 Key in the Slide Title

2 Press [Enter] – a new slide is created

3 Click the Demote tool to move in a level. This takes you to the first bulleted level

4 Key in your first item

5 Press [Enter]. You are positioned below the first item, at the same level

6 Key in your next item

7 Repeat steps 5-6 as necessary

8 Use the Demote or Promote tools to structure you slide as required

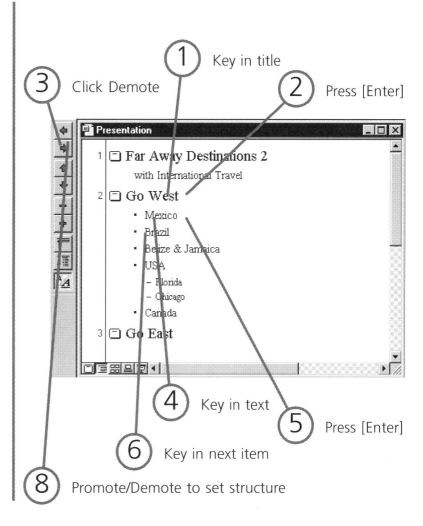

Take note

If the points you are making are to be at a lower level than the first bulleted level, you must demote them - see Promoting & Demoting Points (next page).

Promoting & demoting

The points you want to make on your slides will be structured – you will have main points (at the first bulleted level) and some of these points will have sub-points (at the second, third, fourth or even fifth level).

Initially, all points on your slide are at level 1. You can easily Demote sub items if necessary (and promote them again if you change your mind). Promoting and demoting in Outline view uses the same techniques as in Slide view.

Basic steps

❑ To Demote an item

1 Place the insertion point in the item you wish to Demote

2 Click ⬛ the Demote tool on the Outlining (or Formatting) toolbar

❑ To Promote an item

1 Place the insertion point in the item you wish to Promote

2 Click ⬛ the Promote tool on the Outlining (or Formatting) toolbar

Keyboard Shortcuts

[Shift]-[Alt]- [→]   Demotes an item

[Shift]-[Alt]- [←]   Promotes an item

Take note

You can also click and drag to Demote or Promote points. Move the mouse pointer to the left of the item to be demoted/promoted. Click and drag right (to demote) or left (to promote) until you are at the required level.

Collapse the outline

❏ Collapse selected slides

1 Highlight the set, or place the insertion point anywhere within a single slide

2 Click ⊟ the Collapse Selection tool

❏ To expand again

1 Select the title(s)

2 Click ⊞ the Expand Selection tool

❏ All the slides

1 Click 📃 the Show Titles tool on the Outlining toolbar

2 To expand your presentation again, click 📄 the Show All tool

If you want to get an overview of your presentation, or part of your presentation, you can collapse all (or part of) the outline down to show just the Slide Titles. The outline can then be expanded again to show the text as required.

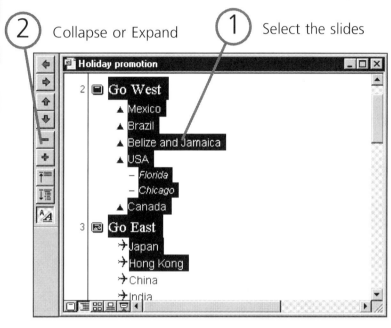

② Collapse or Expand   ① Select the slides

① Show Titles

② Show All

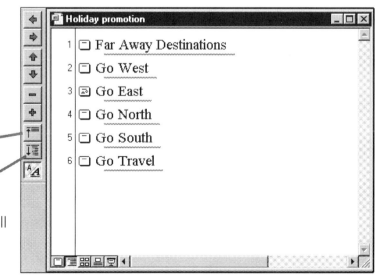

65

Rearranging an outline

If you decide that you want to change the order of the points you have made, this is very easily done in Outline view.

② Move up or down

① Select the item or locate the I-beam

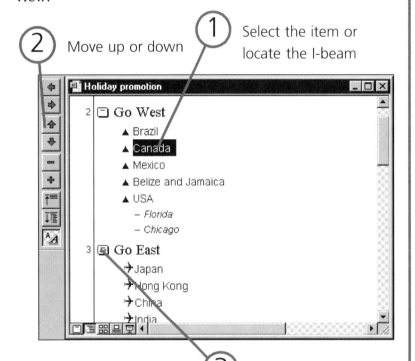

③ Click on the icon

- ❏ Moving items
- 1 Select, or place the insertion point in the item you wish to move
- 2 Click the Move Up tool to move it up through the slide(s)

or

Click the Move Down tool to move it down through the slide(s)

- ❏ Moving slides
- 3 Click on the slide icon to the left of the one you want to move
- 4 Use the tools, mouse or keyboard to move the whole slide to its new location

Take note

You can also click and drag to rearrange points. Move the mouse pointer to the left of the item. Click and drag up or down until the item is in the required position.

Keyboard Shortcuts

[Shift]-[Alt]-[↑] moves an item up

[Shift]-[Alt]-[↓] moves an item down

Deleting slides

1 Click the slide icon on the left of the title to select the slide

2 Press [Delete]

or

3 Open the Edit menu

4 Choose Delete Slide

5 Confirm the deletion by clicking OK

If you need to remove a slide it can easily be deleted in Outline view.

1 Click to select the slide

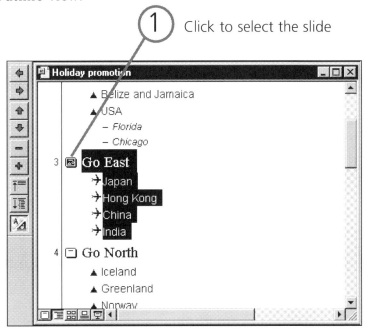

Take note

You can delete slides in Outline view, Slide view, Slide Sorter view or Notes Pages view.

3 Open the Edit menu

4 Choose Delete Slide

5 Click OK to confirm

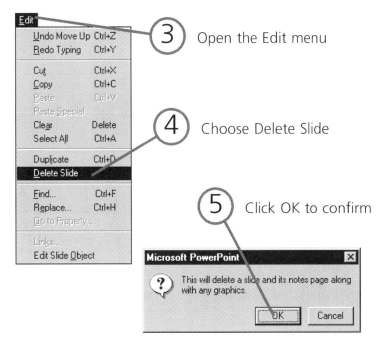

Summary

- ❑ Outline view lets you concentrate on the text and structure of your presentation

- ❑ In Outline view, you can specify the slide title and the points you wish to make on each slide

- ❑ Your points can contain sub-points if necessary (up to 5 levels)

- ❑ You cannot add pictures, charts etc in Outline view

- ❑ Using an outline, you can collapse and expand your presentation to show the slides required

- ❑ You can move between Outline view and the other views whenever you wish

- ❑ You can rearrange the order or delete slides in Outline – or any other – view

7 Drawing

Selecting objects 70

Text tool 72

Drawing tools 73

Free rotate tool 74

AutoShapes 75

Fill, line and shadow 76

Drawing+ toolbar 78

Manipulating objects 79

Summary 82

Selecting objects

So far, we have dealt with Text objects - slide headings and points listed for discussion on the slides.

In this section we are going to consider how the tools on the Drawing toolbar can be used to customise and add interest to your slides. You must be in Slide view for this.

We'll work from the top down!!

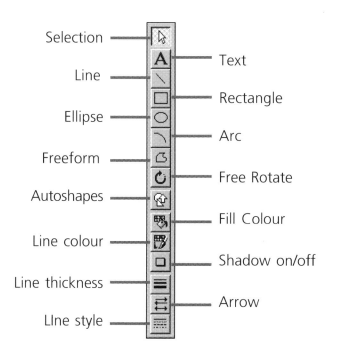

Selection — Line — Ellipse — Freeform — Autoshapes — Line colour — Line thickness — LIne style

Text — Rectangle — Arc — Free Rotate — Fill Colour — Shadow on/off — Arrow

❏ To select a text object

1 Click within the text placeholder area - this places the insertion point within it and shows the grey border

2 Point and click on the border

Note the handles that appear at the corners and along the edges of the selected object.

❏ To select other objects

1 Click anywhere inside the object placeholder

❏ To de-select an object

1 Click anywhere outside the selected object (click inside or outside a text object)

Selection Tool

The Selection tool is used to select objects on your slide. Once an object has been selected, you can move it, resize it, delete it (and lots of other things as we'll soon see). The Selection tool on the Drawing toolbar is always selected unless you pick another tool from the toolbar.

❏ Moving

Point to the *border* of a text object, or anywhere *within* any other type of object (not a handle) and drag it to its new position.

❏ Resizing

Point to one of the handles (note the mouse pointer) and drag it until the object is the required size

❏ Deleting

Press [Delete] on your keyboard

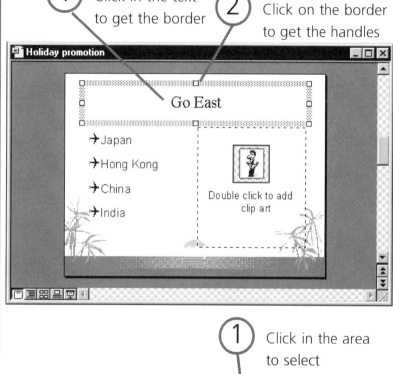

① Click in the text to get the border

② Click on the border to get the handles

Take note

If you delete an object by mistake, click the Undo tool on the Standard toolbar.

① Click in the area to select

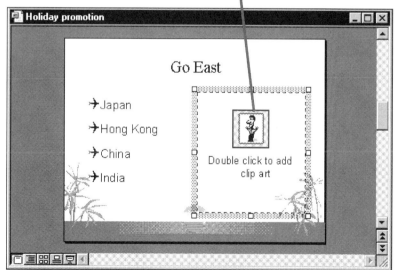

71

Text tool

You can use the text tool to enter text anywhere on your slide (not necessarily within an existing text placeholder).

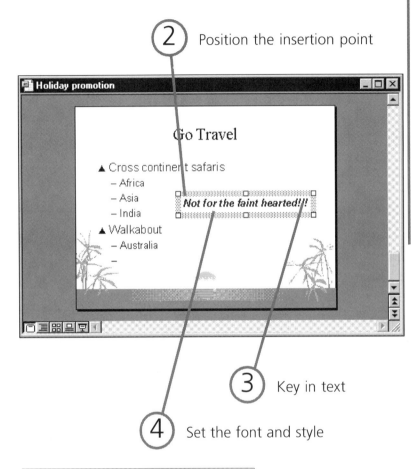

② Position the insertion point

③ Key in text

④ Set the font and style

Basic steps

- ❑ Line based tools
- 1 Select a tool
- 2 Click to set the start
- 3 Drag to draw a shape

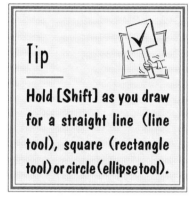

Tip

Hold [Shift] as you draw for a straight line (line tool), square (rectangle tool) or circle (ellipse tool).

- ❑ Freeform tool
- 1 Select ⬚ the Freeform tool
- 2 Click and drag (note the pencil shaped pointer) to draw a line
- 3 Press [Esc] when you are finished to switch the tool off

Tip

Click at each corner of your shape to get straight lines.

Drawing tools

The line, rectangle, ellipse and arc tools all work in a similar way. The more adventurous/artistic among you will have fun with the Freeform tool. Experiment with them on your slides.

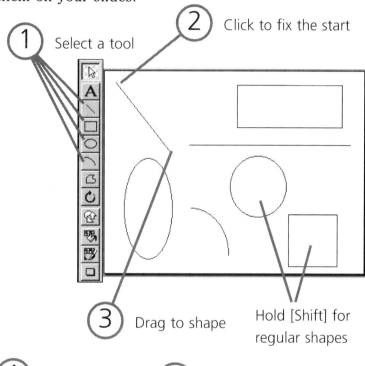

① Select a tool

② Click to fix the start

③ Drag to shape

Hold [Shift] for regular shapes

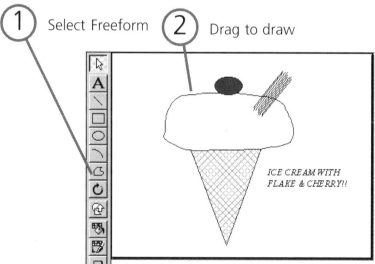

① Select Freeform

② Drag to draw

ICE CREAM WITH FLAKE & CHERRY!!

Free rotate tool

The Free Rotate Tool is used to rotate an object. You can rotate through any angle, in either direction.

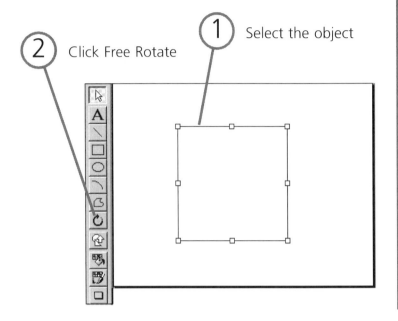

② Click Free Rotate

① Select the object

1 Select the object you want to rotate

2 Click 🖒 the Free Rotate Tool

3 Position the mouse pointer (note its appearance) over one of the handles of the selected object

4 Drag the handle until the object is rotated to its new position

5 Press [Esc] to switch off Free Rotate (or select another tool)

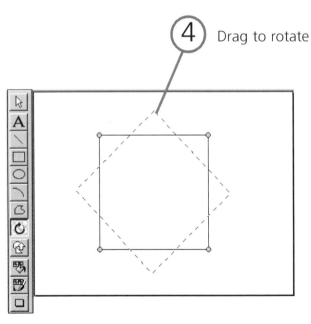

④ Drag to rotate

Mouse pointers

✳ **when over handle**

⊕ **Free Rotate pointer**

AutoShapes

Basic steps

1 Click the AutoShapes tool to display the AutoShapes toolbar

2 Select the shape you want (click on it)

3 Click and drag on your slide to pull the shape to the right size

4 Click the AutoShapes tool to hide the toolbar again

If you want stars, triangles, arrows etc on your slide it's worth looking at the AutoShapes provided. If the shape you want is here, it's a lot easier to use an AutoShape than to draw the design from scratch!

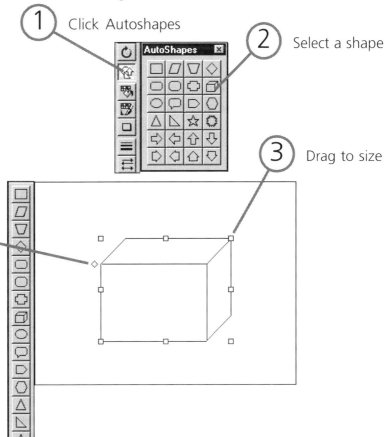

1 Click Autoshapes

2 Select a shape

3 Drag to size

Adjust handle

Take note

On each AutoShape you draw you will notice an adjust handle ◇ Click and drag the handle to adjust the shape of your object.

Tip

If you use the AutoShapes a lot, leave the toolbar showing. You can drag it, by its title bar, to a docking area - top, bottom, right or left of your screen - so it doesn't obscure your slides.

Fill, line and shadow

You can easily change the fill colour/pattern/shading, or the line colour or your object.

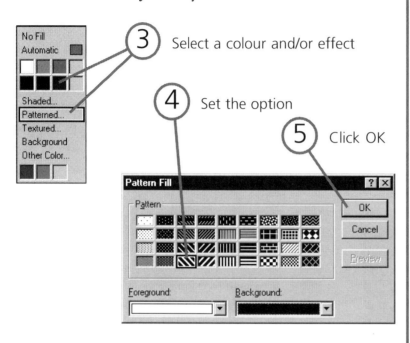

Select a colour and/or effect

Set the option

Click OK

❑ Fill/shading options

1 Select the object

2 Click 🖌 the Fill/ shading tool

3 Select a colour (choose Other Colour... for a larger selection), or go for a shaded, patterned or textured option

4 Choose the effect required

5 Click OK

❑ To change line colour

1 Select the object

2 Click 🖌 the line colour tool

3 Select a colour (choose Other Colour... for a larger selection)

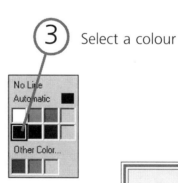

Select a colour

Take note

An object must have a fill colour before you can customise its shading or pattern.

Take note

If you choose Background the selected object takes on the pattern/colour/ shading of the slide background.

Basic steps

Lines and arrowheads

You can select an alternative line style for your object, or if you want to point to something on your slide you can add arrowheads to a line.

❏ Line styles

1 Select your object

2 Click ▤ the Line Style or ▦ Dashed Lines tool

3 Make your choice

❏ Arrowheads

1 Draw your line

2 Select it

3 Click ⇄ the Arrowheads tool

4 Select the arrowhead style you want

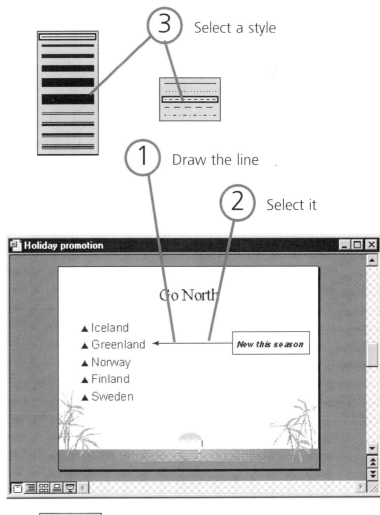

③ Select a style

① Draw the line

② Select it

④ Set the style

Take note

The Shadow tool 🔲 is an on/off toggle. Simply click it to switch the shadow effect on and off. The default setting is for an object to have no shadow.

Drawing+ toolbar

Now that you have used the tools on the Drawing Toolbar, you might like to experiment with the Drawing+ Toolbar!

The Drawing+ Toolbar allows you to pile objects one on top of the other to get special effects, group objects and flip them over! What more could you want!

Display the Drawing+ Toolbar and try out some of the tools.

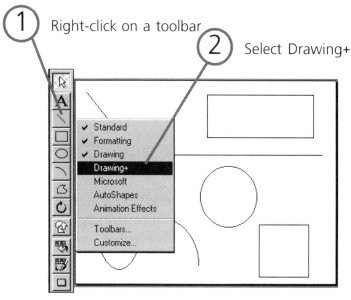

Right-click on a toolbar

Select Drawing+

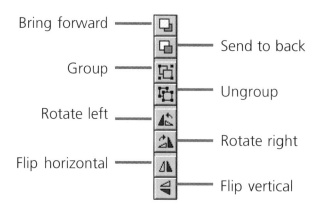

Bring forward ———
Send to back
Group ———
Ungroup
Rotate left ———
Rotate right
Flip horizontal ———
Flip vertical

Basic steps

1 Position the mouse pointer over any toolbar currently displayed and click the right mouse button to display the toolbar shortcut menu

2 Select the Drawing**+** toolbar from the list (click on it)

Take note

In the toolbar shortcut menu, toolbars with a tick beside them are currently displayed.

You can use the menu to switch toolbars on and off, one at a time. If you want to switch several toolbars on or off at the same time, open the View menu and choose Toolbars.

Manipulating objects

Basic steps

1 Select the object you wish to Bring Forward or Send Backward

2 Click 🔳 the Bring Forward or 🔳 Send Backward tool until the object is at the required level

Bring forward, send backward

These tools are useful if you have objects overlapping each other and need to change their relative level. When objects overlap, the first drawn is underneath, and the others are piled on top in the order in which you draw them. You can change the order with the Bring Forward or Send Backward tools.

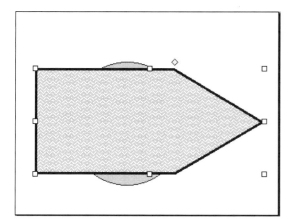

Send the polygon back one level...

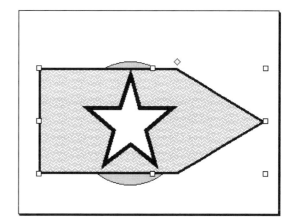

... and again...

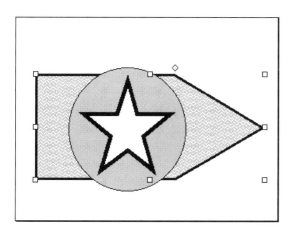

... until the shapes overlap as you want them

Group and ungroup objects

If you have drawn several objects to generate an image, you can group the objects together into one to make it easier to move, copy or resize the whole image.

Should you wish to edit part of the image later, it can be ungrouped back into its original objects.

❑ To group objects

1 Select the objects you want to group

2 Click 🔲 the Group tool

❑ To ungroup objects

1 Select the grouped object

2 Click 🔲 the Ungroup tool

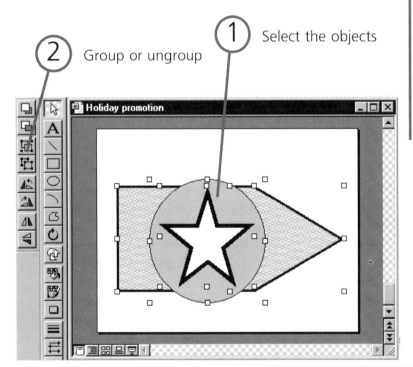

① Select the objects

② Group or ungroup

Take note

To select more than one object:-
Select the first object then hold the [Shift] key down when you select the other objects.

To select all the objects on your slide:-
Press [Ctrl]-[A] or click and drag an outline to include them all.

Basic steps

Rotate and flip

- ❑ To Rotate or Flip
- 1 Select the object
- 2 Click the appropriate Rotate or Flip tool

You can turn an object through 90 degrees left or right with the Rotate tools, or create mirror images with the Flip tools.

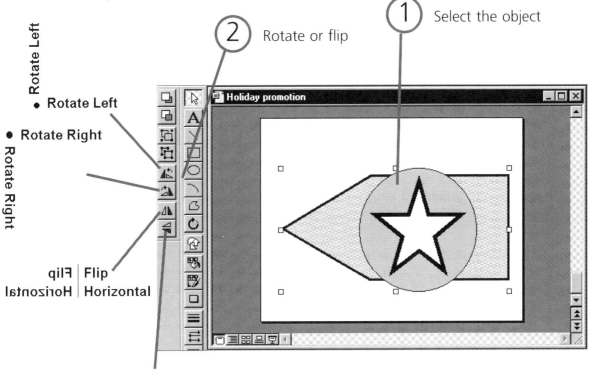

Rotate Left

• **Rotate Left**

• **Rotate Right**

Rotate Right

qilꟻ | **Flip**
lstnosiɿoH | **Horizontal**

ꟻlib Vɘɿɟɿɔɒl
Flip Vertical

Take note

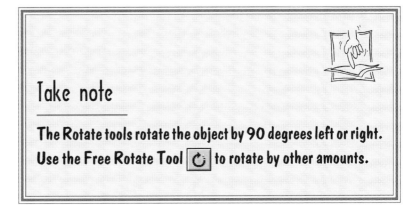

The Rotate tools rotate the object by 90 degrees left or right. Use the Free Rotate Tool to rotate by other amounts.

Summary

- To move, resize or delete an object, you must select it first

- To move a selected object, drag its border

- To resize a selected object, drag one of the handles along its border

- To delete a selected object, press the [Delete] key

- You can use the Line, Rectangle, Ellipse, Arc or Freeform tool to create drawings on your slides

- Objects can be rotated using the Free Rotate and Rotate tools, or mirrored with the Flip tools

- The AutoShapes toolbar contains several useful shapes to add impact to your presentations

- Fill colours, lines and shadows are easily customised

- The Drawing+ toolbar provides many additional features to help you perfect your drawing

8 Graphs

Starting a graph 84

Datasheet and toolbars 86

Chart type 88

Customising graphs 89

Colours and patterns 91

Leaving the graph 93

Summary 94

Starting a graph

There will be times when pictures talk louder than words – and when this is the case you can use graphs, organisation charts, clipart, tables etc to help you make your point. In this section we'll look at ways to add a graph to your slide.

There are 3 main ways to set up your chart using Microsoft Graph:-

- Choose a slide from the New Slide dialog box that has a Graph placeholder already on it

  or

- Choose a slide from the New Slide dialog box that has an Object placeholder already on it

  or

- Click the Insert Graph tool

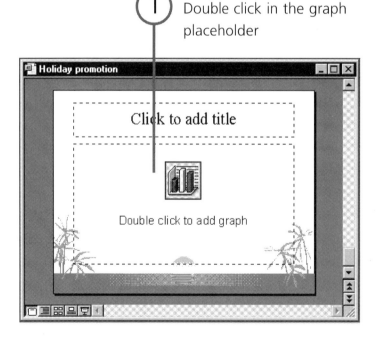

① Double click in the graph placeholder

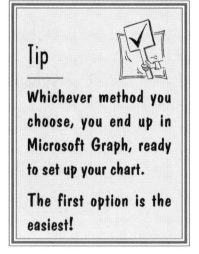

Tip

Whichever method you choose, you end up in Microsoft Graph, ready to set up your chart.

The first option is the easiest!

Basic steps

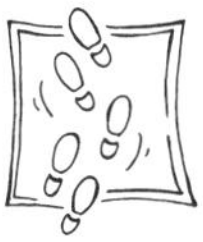

- ❑ Using an Object placeholder

1 Double click within the Object placeholder on your slide to open the Insert Object dialog box

2 Choose Microsoft Graph 5

3 Click OK

1 Double click in the object placeholder

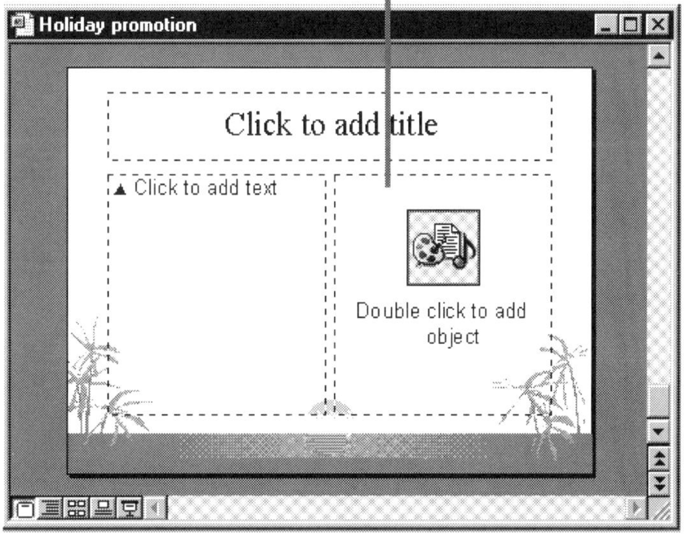

2 Select Microsoft Graph

3 Click OK

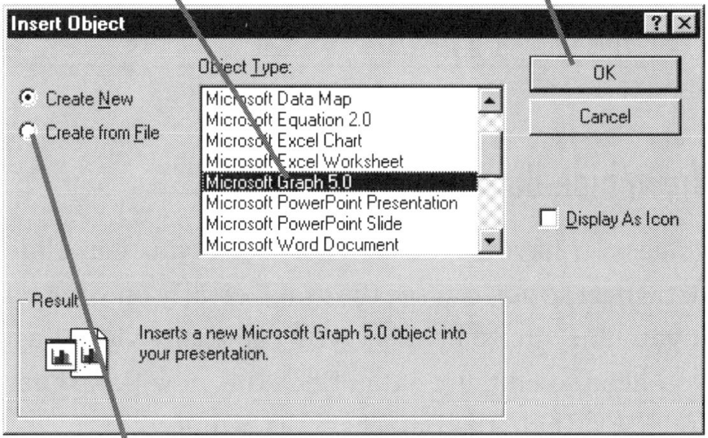

Use the File option to import graphs that you created earlier

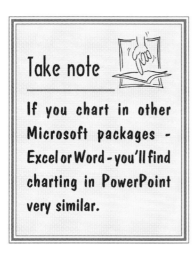

Take note

If you chart in other Microsoft packages - Excel or Word - you'll find charting in PowerPoint very similar.

Datasheet and toolbars

The Graph environment has its own Standard and Drawing toolbars. There is also a small Datasheet window (which can be moved or resized as necessary), where you can key in the data you want to chart.

Entering your own data

You must replace the sample data in the datasheet with the data you want to chart. If you do not need to replace all the sample data, delete the cell contents that are not required – go to the cell and press [Delete].

(1) Move to the cell

(2) Enter your data

‌ Holiday promotion - Datasheet			A	B	C	D
			1st Qtr	2nd Qtr	3rd Qtr	4th Qtr
1		East	20.4	27.4	90	20.4
2		West	30.6	38.6	34.6	31.6
3		North	45.9	46.9	45	43.9
4						

View/hide datasheet

Once you have keyed in your data, you can Hide the datasheet so you can see the graph clearly on your screen. If you hide your datasheet, you can easily view it again if you need to edit any data. Click the view Datasheet tool to view or hide the Datasheet, as required.

Tip

Rather than replacing the sample data cell by cell, it is sometimes quicker— and less confusing – to select and delete all of it, then start again from scratch.

Moving around your datasheet

Tip

Don't enter too much data for charting – this will be presented on a slide or overhead. If it's too detailed your audience may not appreciate it fully!

There are a number of ways to move from cell to cell within the Datasheet. Use the keys:-

Arrow keys	one cell in direction of arrow
[Tab]	forward to the next cell
[Shift]-[Tab]	back to the previous cell
[Enter]	down to the next cell in a column

or

Point to the cell and click.

The cell you are in (your *current* cell) has a dark border.

Standard toolbar

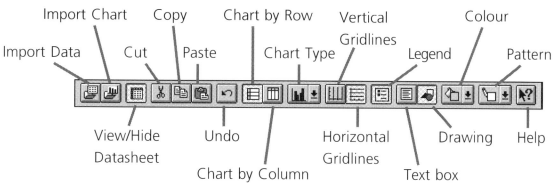

Import Data · Import Chart · Cut · Copy · Paste · Chart by Row · Chart Type · Vertical Gridlines · Legend · Colour · Pattern

View/Hide Datasheet · Undo · Chart by Column · Horizontal Gridlines · Text box · Drawing · Help

Drawing toolbar

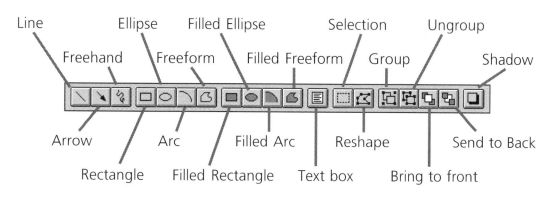

Line · Freehand · Ellipse · Freeform · Filled Ellipse · Filled Freeform · Selection · Group · Ungroup · Shadow

Arrow · Rectangle · Arc · Filled Rectangle · Filled Arc · Text box · Reshape · Bring to front · Send to Back

Chart type

The default chart type is a column chart. You can try out a variety of other chart types using the Chart Type tool on the Standard toolbar.

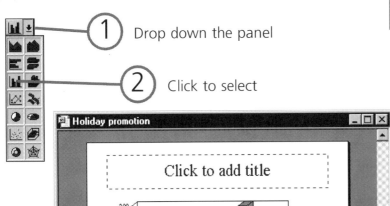

(1) Drop down the panel

(2) Click to select

1 Click the drop down arrow to display the chart types available

2 Choose one

Tip

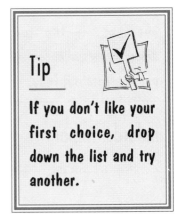

If you don't like your first choice, drop down the list and try another.

Vertical charts (above) are usually more effective than horizontal ones (below)

Area graphs are good for showing cumulative totals and changes over time

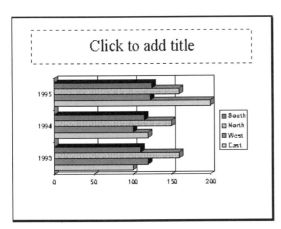

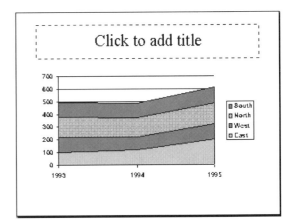

Customising graphs

You can customise the basic chart in a number of different ways, to add your own personal touch.

Gridlines and legends

You can toggle the display of gridlines and legends on your chart with the tools on the Standard toolbar.

- Toggle Vertical Gridlines on and off using
- Toggle Horizontal Gridlines on and off using
- Toggle the Legend on and off using

Vertical Gridlines can make sections clearer in crowded charts

Horizontal Gridlines are useful if you want to point out the values of the bars

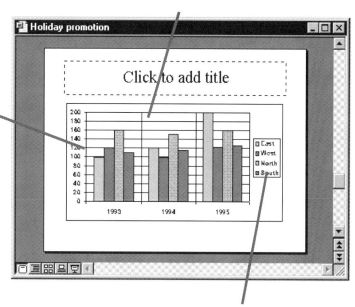

The Legend captions are taken from the headings of the datasheet

Text box

If you want to add text within the chart area, you can use a Text Box for this. The Text Box is a separate object which can be moved, resized or deleted as required.

● If you make your Text Box too large or too small, select it then drag the handles to resize it.

● If you put it in the wrong place, select it then click and drag from within the selected area to move it.

1 Click  the Text Box tool on either toolbar

2 Click and drag to position the text box within the chart area

3 Key in your text

4 Click outside the Text Box to de-select it

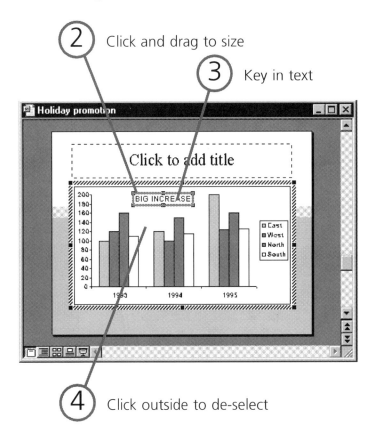

② Click and drag to size

③ Key in text

④ Click outside to de-select

Take note

If you want to change the font style or size, double click on your text box to open the Format Object dialog box. You'll find lots of options to choose from in there!

Colours and patterns

❑ To change colour

1 Select the object

2 Click the drop down
arrow beside the
Colour tool to display
the list of colours you
can choose from

3 Pick a colour

❑ To change patterns

1 Select the object

2 Click the drop down
arrow beside the
Pattern tool to display
the palette of patterns

3 Choose a pattern

If you don't like the colour of the bars (or other objects)
on your chart, or if you want to experiment with patterns
as well as colour, try out the options.

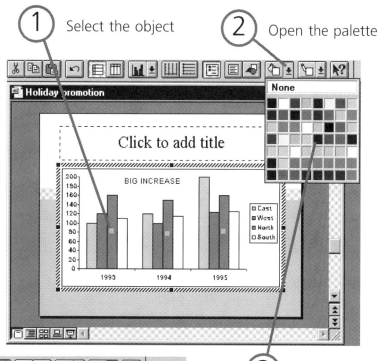

① Select the object

② Open the palette

③ Pick a colour

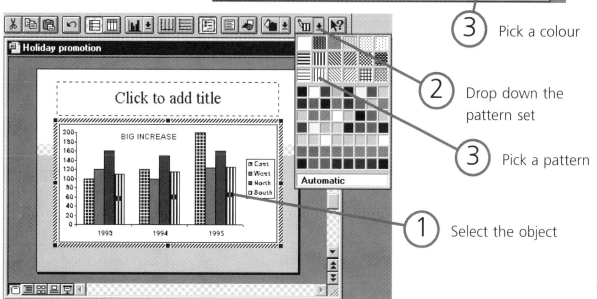

② Drop down the
pattern set

③ Pick a pattern

① Select the object

Format dialog boxes

There is a format dialog box for every type of object in a chart. Double click on any object to open its dialog box, and customise your chart as much as you wish!!

Click on a tab to switch to another panel

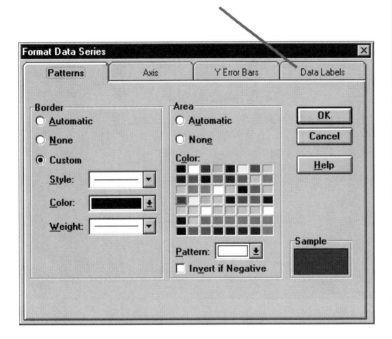

This dialog box opens when you double click on a Data Series (a set of bars or a line on chart.) Other objects have different format dialog boxes to suit their special requirements.

Take note

You can further enhance your charts using the tools on the Drawing toolbar. Toggle it on and off by clicking the Drawing tool on the standard toolbar. Many of the tools are very similar to the ones on the Drawing toolbars in the Slide view.

Leaving the graph

When your chart is complete, click anywhere on the slide outside its placeholder to return to your presentation.

If you wish to take your chart back into the graphic environment, simply double click on it.

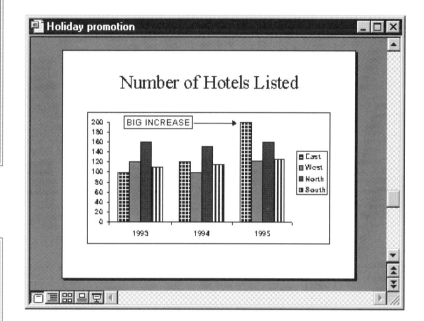

Take note

When you leave the Graph environment, the whole chart becomes an object within your presentation, and can be moved, copied, deleted or resized as necessary.

Take note

Objects created with the Drawing tools can be grouped into a single object. Click on the first, then [Shift] - Click on each other object. Click the Group Objects tool.

To ungroup again, select the grouped object and click the Ungroup Objects tool.

Tip

Before you leave, look through the menus to see what other options Microsoft Graph has to offer - there are plenty.

93

Summary

- ❑ Charts can be used on any of your slides

- ❑ Working in the Graph environment is similar to working and charting in Excel

- ❑ There are several chart types to choose from – bar, line, area etc

- ❑ Colours, patterns, text and drawing can all be used to enhance your charts

- ❑ Double click on any object to open its Format dialog box where you can customise its appearance

- ❑ To leave Graph, and return to your presentation, click anywhere outside the chart placeholder

- ❑ To return an existing chart to the Graph environment, double click on it

9 More objects...

Organisation charts 96

Text and boxes 98

Text and drawing tools 100

Zoom options 102

Finishing touches 103

Update and exit 104

Tables 105

The ClipArt gallery 107

Choosing a picture 108

Media clips 110

Summary 114

Organisation charts

Organisation charts give you another opportunity to make your point using a diagram rather than words.

This section introduces Organisation Chart and some of its features. If you use a lot of organisation charts, tour through its menus and the On-line help to appreciate its full potential.

As with graphs, there are a number of ways to start:

- Choose a slide from the New Slide dialog box that has an Organisation Chart placeholder on it

    or

- Choose a slide with an Object placeholder on it

    or

- Click the Insert Organisation Chart tool

Basic steps

- ❑ With an Organisation Chart placeholder

    1 Double click within the Organisation Chart placeholder on your slide

- ❑ From a slide with no placeholder set

    1 Click the Insert Organisation Chart tool on the standard toolbar

(1) Double click in the chart placeholder

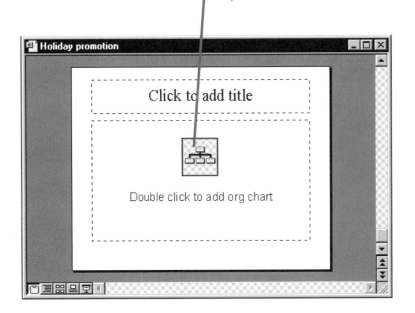

Tip

Work out the structure you wish to display before you start.

96

Basic steps

❑ With an Object placeholder

1 Double click within the Object placeholder on your slide to open the Insert Object dialog box

2 Choose Organisation Chart 2.0

3 Click OK

Tip

Don't try to display too large a structure - the finished slide should be clear and easily understood.

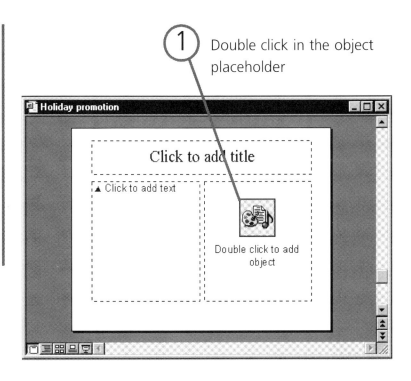

① Double click in the object placeholder

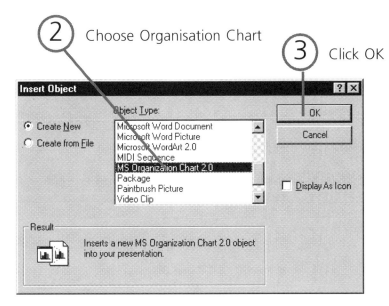

② Choose Organisation Chart

③ Click OK

Text and boxes

The Organisation Chart window

Organisation charts can be very complicated structures but they have only simple elements. The small set of tools in this window are all that you need. Most are for adding boxes, and all the normal range of relationships are covered here.

Selector

Text tool

Zoom

Relationship boxes

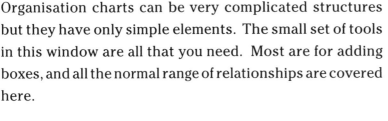

① Click in a box

② Click again to open it

③ Key in your text

④ Click elsewhere to return the box to normal

<Bracketed prompts> are not displayed

Basic steps

❑ To Add a box

1 Select the box type from the Toolbar

2 Click on the box to which the new box is related

3 Type in your text

Adding and deleting boxes

You can easily build your chart up by adding boxes where needed. Deleting boxes is even easier.

① Select a box type

② Click on the related box

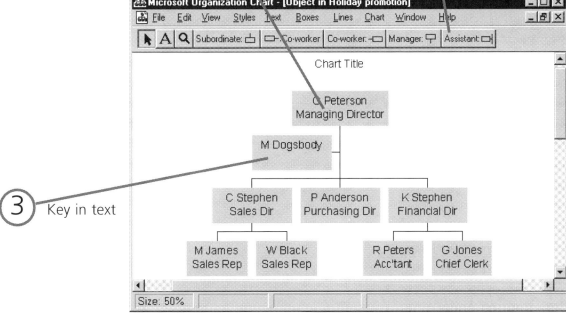

③ Key in text

Take note

You can easily delete a box. Just click on it to select it, and press [Delete]. If you then change your mind, use Edit – Undo to bring it back again.

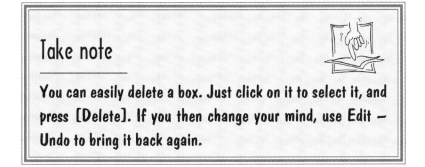

Text and drawing tools

The text and drawing tools can be used to add the finishing touches to your organisation chart. If you need text outside the boxes on your chart, use the Text tool.

☐ Text
1 Click the Text tool
2 Click to position the insertion point
3 Key in the text
4 Click anywhere outside the text area to deselect the text

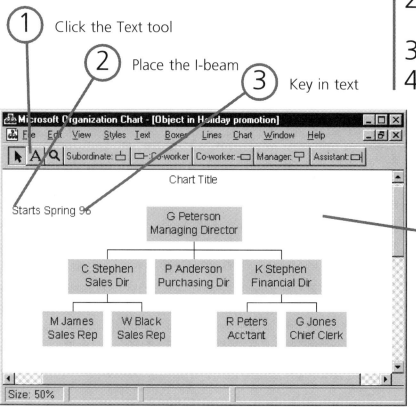

1 Click the Text tool

2 Place the I-beam

3 Key in text

4 Click anywhere

The Drawing tools

There are only four drawing tools for the Chart – three types of line and a box.

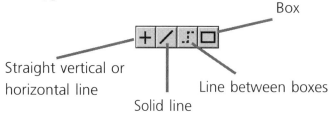

Box

Straight vertical or horizontal line

Line between boxes

Solid line

☐ Drawing
1 Press [Ctrl]–[D] to toggle the display of the drawing tools
2 Select a tool
3 Click and drag to draw a line or box

100

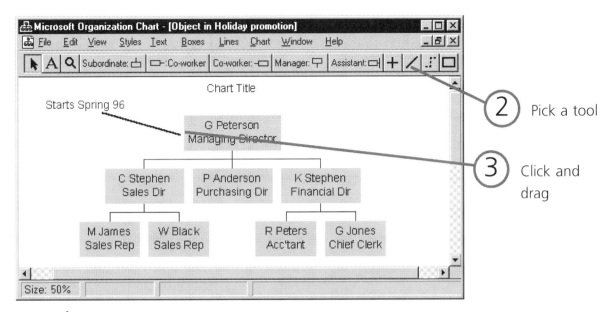

2 Pick a tool

3 Click and drag

Basic steps

1 Select the Chart Title prompt

2 Either key in the title

or

Press [Delete] to remove the title prompt

Chart title

You can give your chart a title here or in the Slide Title area, back in your presentation. If you opt to key in the title in the presentation, delete the Chart Title prompt.

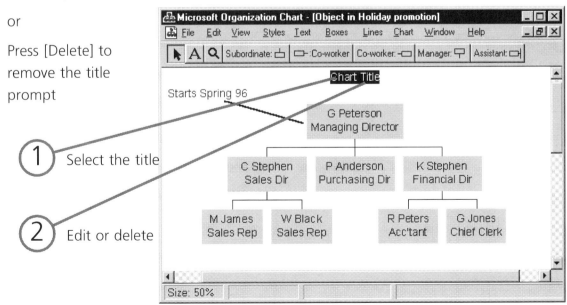

1 Select the title

2 Edit or delete

Zoom options

You can zoom in and out on your organisation chart to get a closer look at what's there, or to get an overview of the whole thing. There are 4 options:-

● Size to Window – for an overview of the whole chart

● 50% of Actual – the best mode for normal work

● Actual Size (100%) – in this mode the Zoom tool toggles to Size to Window

● 200% of Actual – if you want to get really close

Click to Zoom out – the button toggles back to 🔍

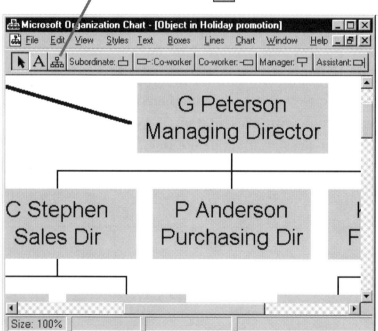

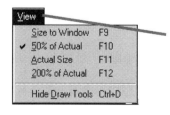

You can get to all screen options from the View menu or the [F] keys.

Basic steps

❏ Zoom to Actual size

1 Click 🔍 the Zoom tool

2 Click on the place on the chart that you want to zoom in on

❏ Zoom out

1 Select ⬚ the Size to Window tool

2 Click on the chart – the whole thing reduces so you can see the entire chart in your window.

❏ Return to Normal

1 Open the View Menu

2 Select 50% of Actual

Keyboard shortcuts

[F9] Size to Window

[F10] 50% of Actual

[F11] Actual Size

[F12] 200% of Actual Size

Basic steps

□ To restyle a box

1 Select the box(es) you want to edit

2 Open the Boxes menu and choose Border, Shadow or Colour as required

3 Select an option from the set displayed

□ To edit lines

1 Select the line(s) you want to edit

2 From the Lines menu choose Thickness, Style or Colour

3 Set the style or colour

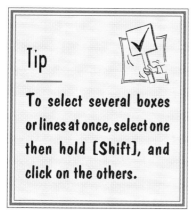
Finishing touches

Using the Boxes, Lines and Text menus, you can add the finishing touches to your organisation chart - edit the line styles, add shadows to the boxes, change the colour, size and font of text etc.

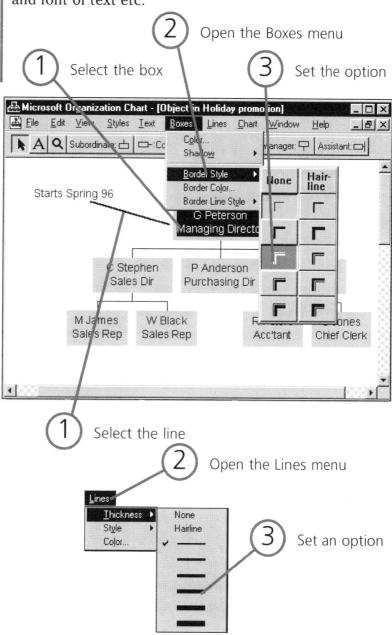

② Open the Boxes menu

① Select the box

③ Set the option

① Select the line

② Open the Lines menu

③ Set an option

Update and exit

Once you've completed your organisation chart, you will need to update the slide in your presentation and return to the presentation proper to continue working on it.

Exit Organisation Chart as you do any Windows application.

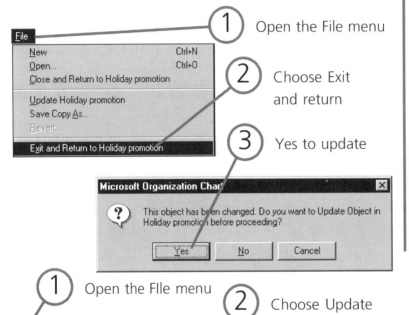

(1) Open the File menu

(2) Choose Exit and return

(3) Yes to update

1 Open the File Menu

2 Choose Exit and Return to *presentation name*

3 Click Yes to update your presentation, before exiting

or

1 Open the File menu

2 Choose Update *presentation name*

   Your slide will now display your chart.

3 Click the Close button on the title bar

(1) Open the FIle menu

(2) Choose Update

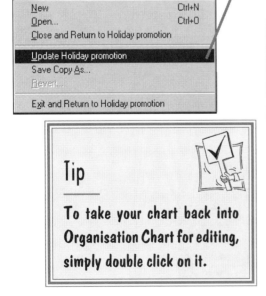

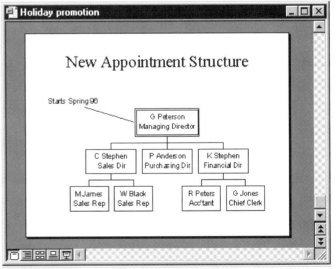

Tip

To take your chart back into Organisation Chart for editing, simply double click on it.

Basic steps

❏ Slide with placeholder

1 Double click on the Table placeholder on your slide

2 Specify the number of rows and columns

❏ From a slide with no table placeholder

1 Open the Insert menu and choose Microsoft Word Table

2 Specify the number of rows and columns

Tables

If you are accustomed to creating tables using Word, you'll find it very easy to create tables on your slides.

There are several ways to get started. You could

● Create a new slide with a Table placeholder set up

● Use the Insert Word Table tool on the standard toolbar

● Choose Microsoft Word Table from the Insert menu

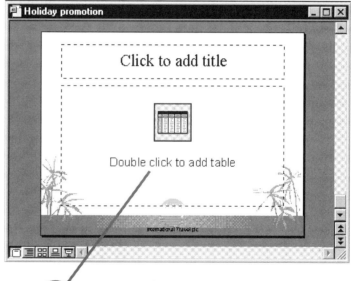

① Double click in the placeholder

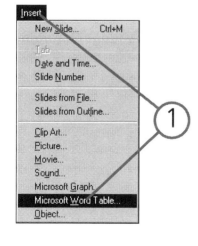

① Use Insert – Word Table

② Set the table size

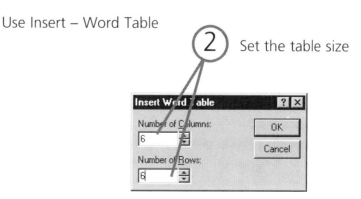

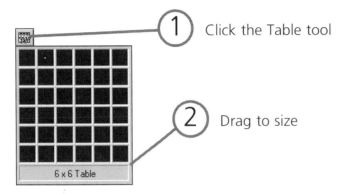

① Click the Table tool

② Drag to size

6 x 6 Table

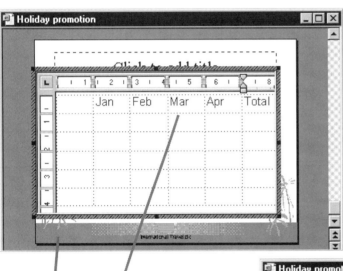

③ Key in and format data

④ Click outside when done

- [ ] Using the Table button

1 Click [▦] the Insert Word Table tool

2 Click and drag over the grid to specify the table size required

- [ ] Entering data

3 Complete your table using the usual Word tools and menus

4 Click outside the table area when done

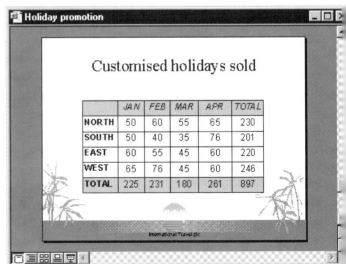

Customised holidays sold

	JAN	FEB	MAR	APR	TOTAL
NORTH	50	60	55	65	230
SOUTH	50	40	35	76	201
EAST	60	55	45	60	220
WEST	65	76	45	60	246
TOTAL	225	231	180	261	897

Basic steps

❑ From a slide with a ClipArt placeholder

1 Double click within the ClipArt placeholder

❑ From a slide with an Object placeholder

1 Double click within the Object placeholder to open the Insert Object dialog box

2 Choose Microsoft ClipArt Gallery

3 Click OK

❑ From a slide with no placeholder set

1 Click 🖾 the Insert ClipArt tool on the standard toolbar

PowerPoint comes with a lot of ClipArt pictures that can be added to your slides. There are three main ways of getting your hands (or mouse) on the ClipArt.

● Set up a New Slide with a ClipArt placeholder on it

or

● Choose a slide from the New Slide dialog box that has an Object placeholder already on it

or

● Click the Insert ClipArt tool

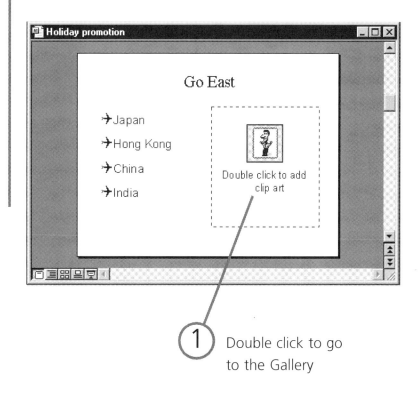

① Double click to go to the Gallery

Take note

However you start, you end up Microsoft ClipArt Gallery, ready to choose your picture.

Choosing a picture

The ClipArt is organised into several categories to make it easier for you to locate pictures. Browse through them to see what is available. Once you have selected the category, thumbnail images are displayed in the Pictures: window. Simply choose the one that best suits your purposes.

Basic steps

1 Scroll through the Categories: to find a set

2 Click on the Category name to select it

3 Scroll through the Pictures until you see the one you want

4 Click on the picture to select it

5 Click Insert

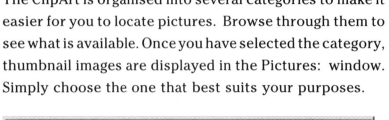

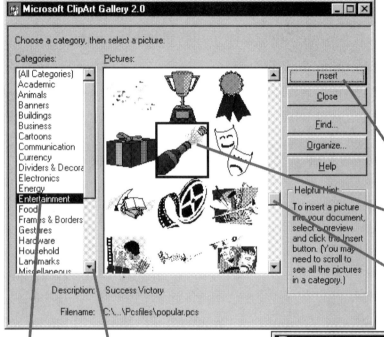

(5) Insert it

(4) Select a picture

(3) See what's there

(1) Scroll through the Categories

(2) Click to select

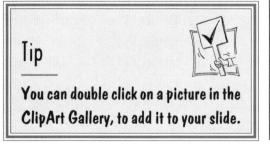

Tip

You can double click on a picture in the ClipArt Gallery, to add it to your slide.

Fine tuning the picture

The picture can be edited in the same way as any other object on your slide.

After you have clicked on a picture to select it, you can..

●   Press [Delete] to delete the object

●   Click and drag any of the handles around the edges of the picture to resize it

●   Click and drag the edge (not a handle) of the picture to move it

Deselect it by clicking anywhere off it.

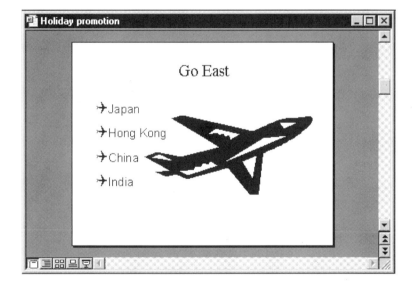

Tip

Use the ClipArt, Drawing and Text tools to create less formal slides!

How about a themed approach? On this slide, the ClipArt plane has been matched by use of the Wingding ✈ as the bullet character.

Media clips

If your computer has multi-media capabilities, you might want to consider adding music to your presentation.

There are several sounds and short pieces supplied with Microsoft Office which may be useful, or you could include a track or two from a CD.

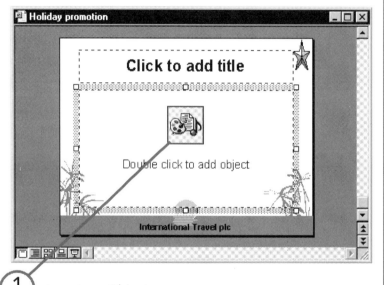

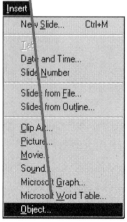

1 Insert an Object

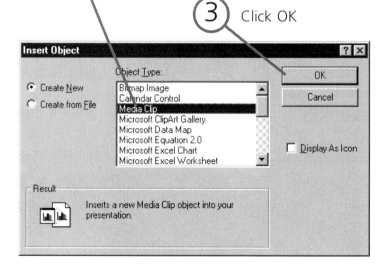

2 Select Media Clip

3 Click OK

❑ A slide with a Media Clip placeholder

1 Double click the Media Clip placeholder

❑ A slide with an Insert Object placeholder

1 Double click the Object placeholder

2 Select Media Clip from the dialog box

3 Click [OK]

❑ A slide with no placeholder

1 Open the Insert menu and choose Object...

2 Select Media Clip

3 Click [OK]

Sound and MIDI Sequencer Clips

1 Open the Insert Clip
   menu
2 Select the type of clip
   required – Sound or
   MIDI Sequencer will
   display those supplied
   with Microsoft Office
3 Pick the one required
4 Click [Open]
5 Click anywhere outside
   the object placeholder
   to return to your
   presentation

You must now decide which clip you wish to insert. There are Sound and MIDI Sequencer Clips supplied with Microsoft Office (or you might prefer to use a clip from a CD – see next page.)

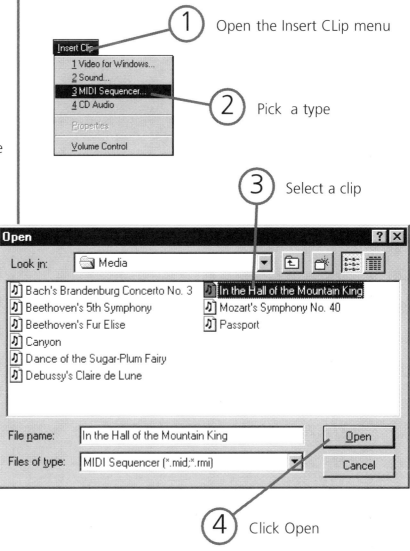

① Open the Insert CLip menu

② Pick a type

③ Select a clip

④ Click Open

CD Clips

Insert your CD before you start. If your CD starts to play automatically, open the CD Player window, stop the track and *close* the CD application window (don't simply minimise it).

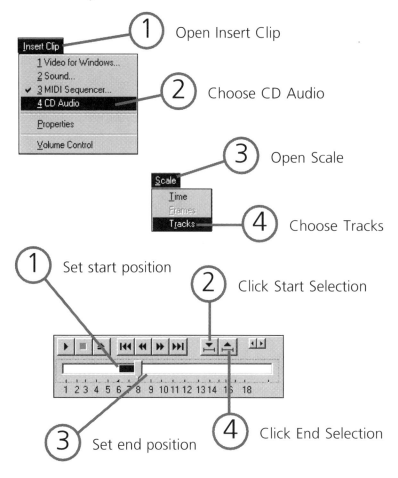

① Open Insert Clip

② Choose CD Audio

③ Open Scale

④ Choose Tracks

① Set start position

② Click Start Selection

③ Set end position

④ Click End Selection

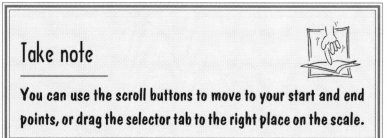

Take note

You can use the scroll buttons to move to your start and end points, or drag the selector tab to the right place on the scale.

Basic steps

1 Open the Insert Clip menu

2 Choose CD Audio

3 Open the Scale menu

4 Choose Tracks to display the tracks on your CD

❑ To select your track(s)

1 Set your chosen start position by clicking on the white bar, until the selector tab is at the track you want to start on

2 Click the Start Selection tool

3 Set your chosen finish position by clicking on the white bar, until the selector tab is at the track you want to end on

4 Click the End Selection tool

5 Click anywhere outside the object placeholder to return to your presentation

To play your clip

☐ In slide view
1 Double click on the
   object

☐ In a slide show
1 Click on the object

You can play your clip in either slide view, or during a slide show on your computer

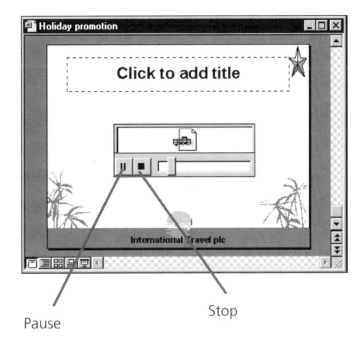

Pause

Stop

Take note

You can pause or stop the playback using the media controls on the slide.

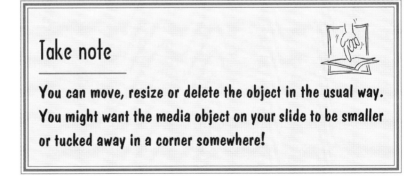

Take note

You can move, resize or delete the object in the usual way. You might want the media object on your slide to be smaller or tucked away in a corner somewhere!

Summary

- ❏ Organisation Charts can easily be added to your slides

- ❏ Boxes are added to and deleted from organisation charts as required

- ❏ Text and drawing tools are available to further enhance your chart

- ❏ There are several Zoom options so you can get a close up look or an overview of your chart

- ❏ The colour and format of items on your chart can be controlled from the Boxes and Text menus

- ❏ Remember to Update your presentation before exiting the Organisation Chart

- ❏ Word Tables can be created on your slides very easily

- ❏ Word menus and toolbars are used when working on your table in PowerPoint

- ❏ The simplest way to add ClipArt is to start with a slide that has a ClipArt placeholder

- ❏ The ClipArt gallery contains over 1000 pictures, arranged in several categories

- ❏ Double click on the picture you want in the ClipArt Gallery dialog box to insert it onto your slide

- ❏ You can move, resize or delete the ClipArt object once it is on your slide

- ❏ Double click on your ClipArt object to return to the Gallery if you wish to choose a different picture

- ❏ You can easily add CD or other sound clips into your presentation.

10 Masters

Slide master .116

Title master .118

Handout master 119

Notes master 121

Summary 122

Slide master

The Slide Master holds the formatted placeholders for the slide title and text. Changes to the Slide Master will be reflected in every slide that follows the slide master format. Any slides where you have made changes to the text formatting at slide level will be treated as exceptions and will retain the custom formatting you applied to them (unless you go back and change it).

Any background objects you want to appear on every slide (like your company name or logo) should be added to the Slide Master.

1 Choose Master from the View menu

2 Select Slide Master

3 Amend the Slide Master as required (using the same techniques you use on a slide in your presentation)

4 Choose an alternative view to leave your Slide Master

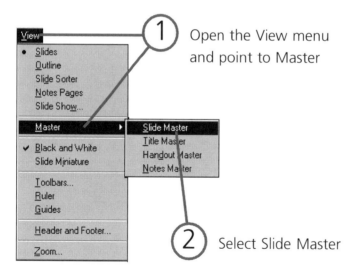

Open the View menu and point to Master

Select Slide Master

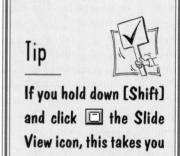

Tip

If you hold down [Shift] and click ▢ the Slide View icon, this takes you to the Slide Master, or to the Title Master (next page) if you are on the title slide at the time.

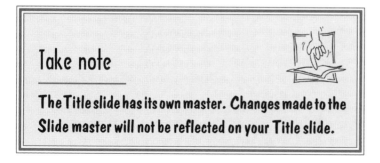

Take note

The Title slide has its own master. Changes made to the Slide master will not be reflected on your Title slide.

③ Amend the master slide

Font changed

ClipArt added

Formatting changed

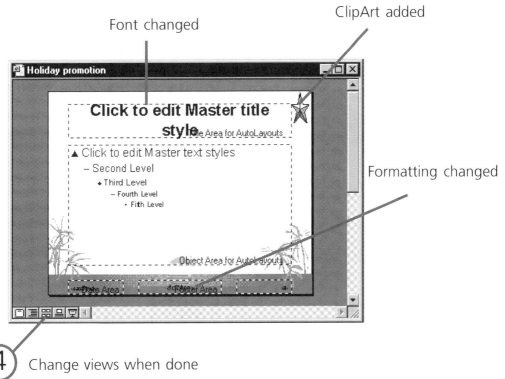

④ Change views when done

Take note

Masters can only be accessed when a presentation is open.

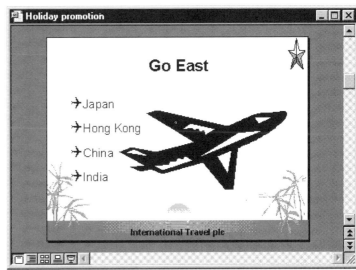

Title master

You can view and edit the Title Master if you wish. Changes made to the Title Master will only affect the title slide, not the others in the presentation.

Basic steps

1 Choose Master from the View menu

2 Select Title Master

3 Amend the Title Master as required (using the same techniques you use on a slide in your presentation)

4 Choose an alternative view to leave your Title Master

③ Edit Title Master

Font changed   ClipArt added

④ Change views to end

Tip

You can drag the elevator to move from the slide master to the title master view.

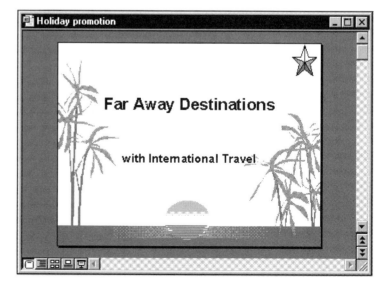

118

Basic steps

1 Choose Master from the View menu

2 Select Handout Master

3 Amend the Handout Master as required (using the same techniques you use on a slide in your presentation)

4 Choose an alternative view to leave your Handout master

You can support your presentation with audience handouts if you wish. Handouts consist of smaller, printed versions of your slides, either 2, 3 or 6 to the page (see section 12 for details on printing).

If you want additional information on the handout pages – your company name or logo, the presentation title, page numbers, date, or lines for your audience to write on – add the detail to the Handout Master.

③ Edit Handout Master

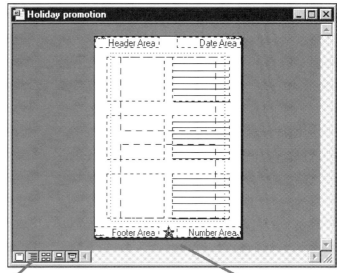

④ Change views when done

ClipArt added

Take note

Look carefully at the master – if you print 2 slides to the page, the 2 large placeholders will contain the slide images. At 3 slides to the page, the 3 placeholders down the left are used. At 6 slides to the page the placeholders down the left and right side are used.

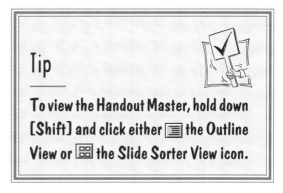

Tip

To view the Handout Master, hold down [Shift] and click either ▤ the Outline View or ▦ the Slide Sorter View icon.

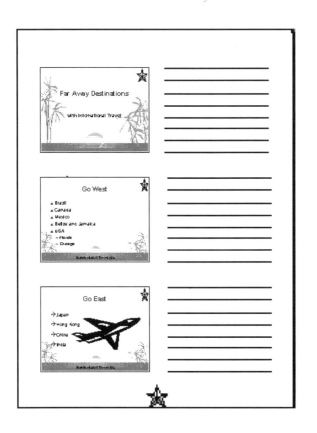

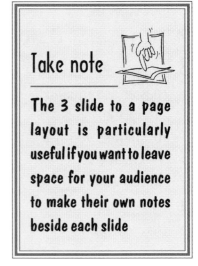

Take note

The 3 slide to a page layout is particularly useful if you want to leave space for your audience to make their own notes beside each slide

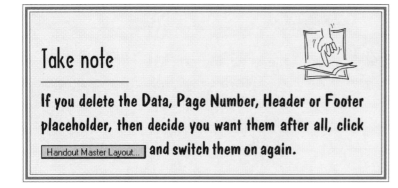

Take note

If you delete the Data, Page Number, Header or Footer placeholder, then decide you want them after all, click Handout Master Layout... and switch them on again.

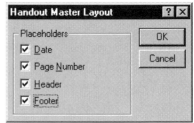

Basic steps

1 Choose Master from the View menu
2 Select Notes Master
3 Amend the Notes Master as required
4 Choose an alternative view to leave your Notes Master

Each slide in your presentation has an accompanying notes page which consists of a smaller version of the slide along with room for any notes you want to make.

If you want to add information to your notes pages (company name or page number perhaps), or change the size of the placeholders (to allow more space for notes and less for the slide image) do so on the Notes Master.

③ Edit Notes Master

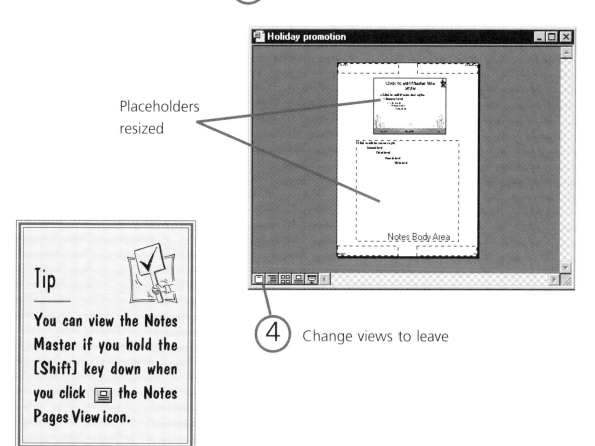

Placeholders resized

Notes Body Area

④ Change views to leave

Tip

You can view the Notes Master if you hold the [Shift] key down when you click 🖳 the Notes Pages View icon.

Summary

- [ ] If you want to add or amend an element to every slide (except the title slide) in your presentation, change the Slide Master, not the individual slides

- [ ] If you want to add or amend an element to the Title slide, change the Title Master, not the individual slide

- [ ] Text, graphics, page numbers, time and date fields added to the Slide, Outline, Handouts and Notes Masters appear on every slide or page

- [ ] Hold the [Shift] key down when you click the View icons to get the Masters

11 Slide Shows

Slide sorter view 124

Hide slide 125

Transitions .126

Build 128

Rehearse Timings 130

Slide Show .132

Slide Show options 135

Summary 136

Slide sorter view

Slide Sorter view was introduced in Section 5 where we considered how you could rearrange the order of your slides. There are several other useful features worth exploring in Slide Sorter view, including:-

● Hiding slides

● Setting up transitions

● Building slides

● Rehearsing timings

We'll look at these features in this section, and see how they can help enhance your presentations.

You should be in Slide Sorter view for this section.

Take note

The topics introduced in this section are only useful if you will be giving on-screen presentations (a slide show). They do not apply to overheads and 35mm slides.

Slide Sorter toolbar

Transition   Build effects   Rehearse timings

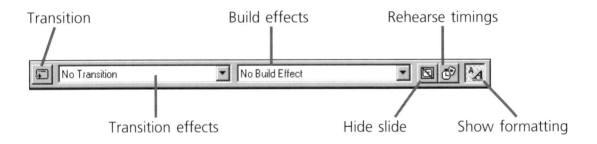

Transition effects   Hide slide   Show formatting

Take note

Transitions, Builds and Hiding Slides can be specified in any view using the Tools menu, but I find it easiest to do them from Slide Sorter view using the Slide Sorter toolbar.

Basic steps

1 Select the slide you want to hide

2 Click 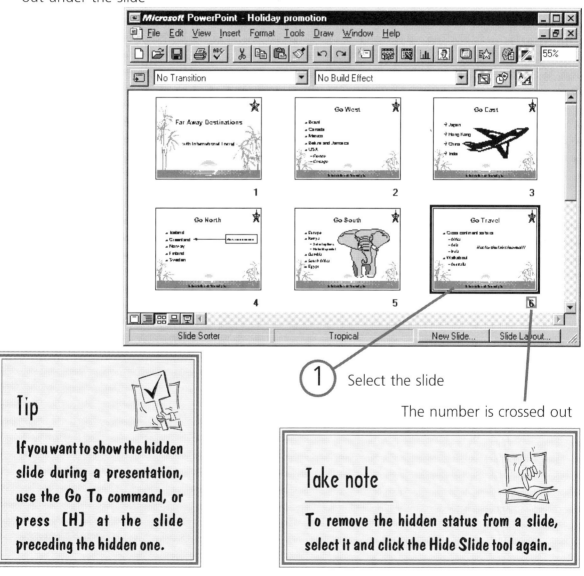 the Hide Slide tool

❏ The number is crossed out under the slide

Hide slide

This option can prove useful if you're not sure whether or not you will really need a particular slide for your presentation. You can include the slide in your presentation (in case it's needed), but hide it. The hidden slide will be by-passed during your slide show, unless you decide you need to use it.

① Select the slide

The number is crossed out

Tip

If you want to show the hidden slide during a presentation, use the Go To command, or press [H] at the slide preceding the hidden one.

Take note

To remove the hidden status from a slide, select it and click the Hide Slide tool again.

Transitions

A transition is an effect used between slides in a slide show. The default option is that No Transition is set, but there are several interesting alternatives you might find effective for your presentation. Experiment with the Transition options until you discover those best suited to your presentation.

Basic steps

1 Select the slide to which you want to specify a transition

2 Click the Transition tool

3 Select the Effect from the drop down list

4 The Preview window demonstrates the effect – click on it to see the effect again

5 Set the Speed to Fast. Focus your audiences on your slides, not the transition method!

6 Choose an Advance option

7 Add a Sound if wanted

8 Click OK

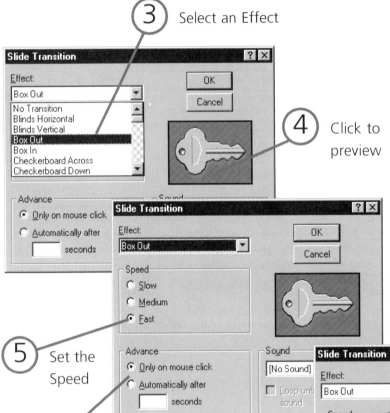

③ Select an Effect

④ Click to preview

⑤ Set the Speed

⑥ Automatic or mouse Advance?

⑦ Sound effect?

⑧ Click OK

This icon shows that a transition is set.
Click on it to see the transition effect.

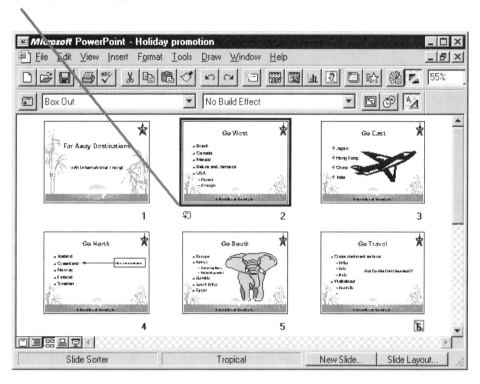

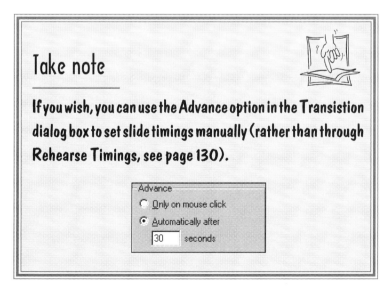

Take note

If you wish, you can use the Advance option in the Transistion dialog box to set slide timings manually (rather than through Rehearse Timings, see page 130).

Build

Basic steps

If you have several points listed on your slide, you could try "building" the slide up during the presentation, rather than presenting the whole list at once. Experiment with the Build options and effects until you find the ones you prefer.

1 Select the slide
2 Drop down the Build Effect list
3 Choose an effect

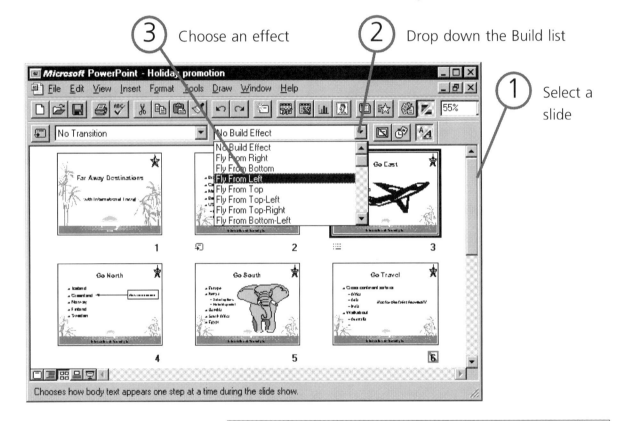

Choose an effect

Drop down the Build list

Select a slide

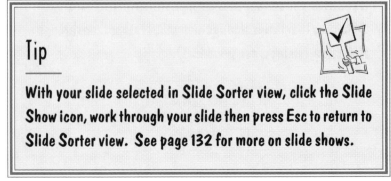

Tip

With your slide selected in Slide Sorter view, click the Slide Show icon, work through your slide then press Esc to return to Slide Sorter view. See page 132 for more on slide shows.

Build options

1 Select the slide
2 Open the Tools menu
3 Choose Build Slide Text
  – Other...
4 Specify the options
  required
5 Click OK

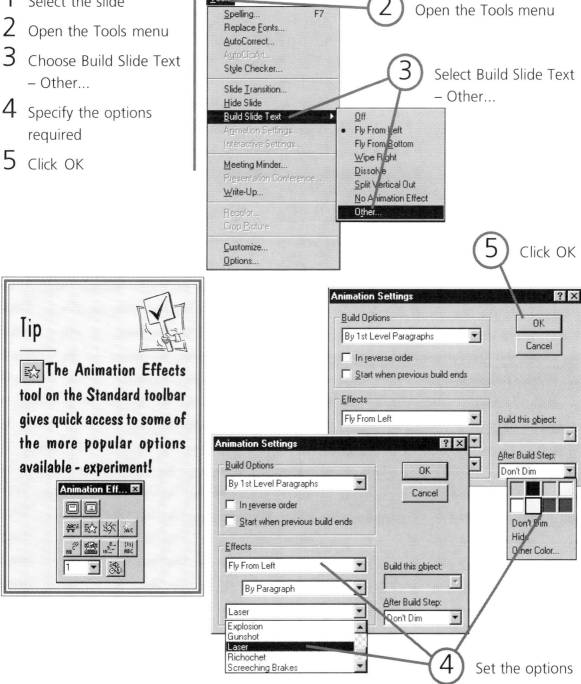

② Open the Tools menu

③ Select Build Slide Text
   – Other...

⑤ Click OK

Tip

📖☆ **The Animation Effects
tool on the Standard toolbar
gives quick access to some of
the more popular options
available - experiment!**

④ Set the options

129

Rehearse Timings

It is a very good idea to practise your presentation before you end up in front of your audience. As well as practising what you intend to say (probably with the aid of notes you have made using the Notes Pages feature), you can rehearse the timings for each slide.

1 Click 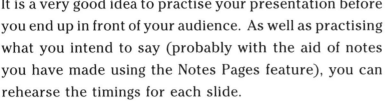 the Rehearse Timings tool to go into your slide show for a practise run!

2 Go over what you intend to say while the slide is displayed

3 Click the left mouse button to move to the next slide when ready

4 Repeat steps 2 and 3 until you reach the end of your presentation

Total presentation time

Current slide timing

Rehearsal

00:01:37   00:00:17

Repeat   ❚❚   ▷

Start slide timing again

Pause

Play

(1) Click Rehearse Timings

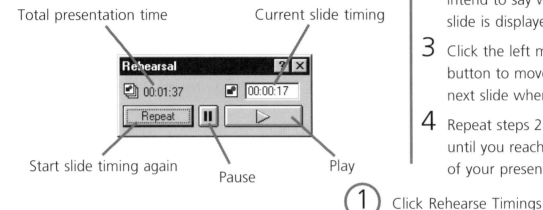

Microsoft PowerPoint - Holiday promotion

File Edit View Insert Format Tools Draw Window Help

No Transition   Fly From Left   55%

Far Away Destinations	Go West	Go East
1	2	3
Go North	Go South	Go Travel
4	5	6

Slide Sorter   Tropical   New Slide...   Slide Layout...

Displaying timings

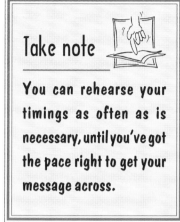

Take note

You can rehearse your timings as often as is necessary, until you've got the pace right to get your message across.

A dialog box displays the total length of time your presentation took and asks if you want the individual slide times recorded under each slide in Slide Sorter view. If you choose yes, the timings are displayed under the slides.

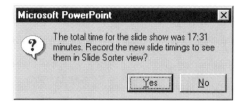

Slide timings

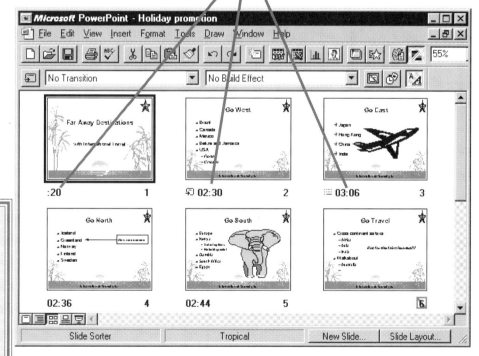

Tip

You can set your timings manually in the Transition dialog box. See page 126.

Slide Show

You can run your slide show at any time to check how your presentation is progressing. Each slide fills the whole of your computer screen. After the last, you are returned to the view you were in when you clicked the Slide Show tool.

1. Select the slide to start from, usually the first

2. Click 📺 the Slide Show tool to the left of the scroll bar

3. Press [PageDown] (or click the left mouse button) to move onto the next slide

   Press [PageUp] to move back to the previous slide if necessary

   Press [Esc] to exit your slide show at any time

Select the starting slide

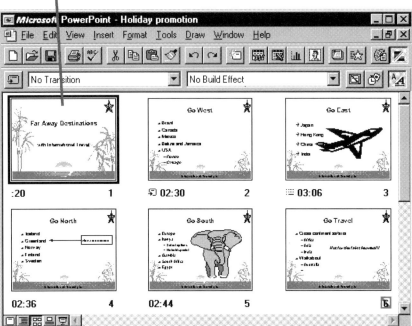

Click Slide Show

Tip

Use the Slide Show in Slide Sorter view when experimenting with Transition and Build effects. Then you can check that the options you choose are having the desired effect.

Basic steps

1 Click the right mouse button or 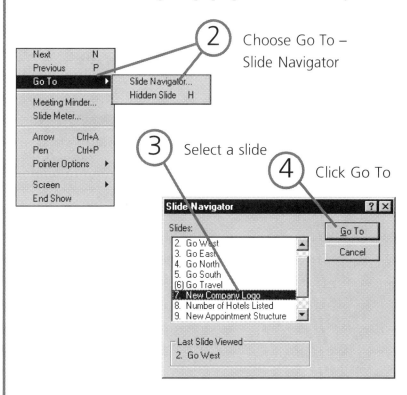 the pop-up menu icon at the bottom left corner of the screen

❑ To go directly to a slide

2 Select Go To, then Slide Navigator

3 Choose the slide you want to go to

4 Click Go To

❑ To 'draw' on the slides

5 Select Pen from the menu or press [Ctrl]-[P] to change the mouse pointer to a pen

6 Click and drag to draw

7 Select Arrow from the menu or press [Ctrl]-[A] to change back to the mouse pointer again

❑ To erase your drawing

8 Press [E] on your keyboard.

Working within your slide show

When presenting your slide show, you might want to leave the normal sequence, go directly to a slide, or draw on the slide to focus attention. These, and other features can be accessed using the pop-up menu or the keyboard.

Choose Go To – Slide Navigator

Select a slide

Click Go To

Take note

You can Blackout your screen by pressing [B] or Whiteout your screen by pressing [W]. This could prove useful while you explain something, or show your audience something. Simply press [B] or [W] again to restore the slide view.

Take note

To get more help on the options available to you while running your slide show, press [F1]. The slide show Help dialog box lists other options you might want to experiment with.

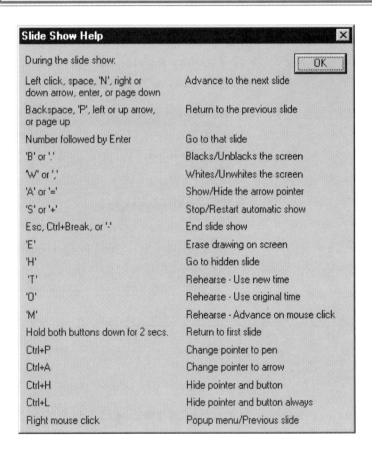

Slide Show Help ☒

During the slide show: [OK]

Left click, space, 'N', right or down arrow, enter, or page down	Advance to the next slide
Backspace, 'P', left or up arrow, or page up	Return to the previous slide
Number followed by Enter	Go to that slide
'B' or '.'	Blacks/Unblacks the screen
'W' or ','	Whites/Unwhites the screen
'A' or '='	Show/Hide the arrow pointer
'S' or '+'	Stop/Restart automatic show
Esc, Ctrl+Break, or '-'	End slide show
'E'	Erase drawing on screen
'H'	Go to hidden slide
'T'	Rehearse - Use new time
'O'	Rehearse - Use original time
'M'	Rehearse - Advance on mouse click
Hold both buttons down for 2 secs.	Return to first slide
Ctrl+P	Change pointer to pen
Ctrl+A	Change pointer to arrow
Ctrl+H	Hide pointer and button
Ctrl+L	Hide pointer and button always
Right mouse click	Popup menu/Previous slide

Tip

Experiment with the pop-up menu and read the Slide Show Help screen to find what options are available.

Basic steps

1 Choose Slide Show from the View menu

2 Set the range of slides

3 Specify the Advance method required

4 Select the Loop Continuously Until "Esc" if you want your presentation to run continuously

5 Click Show

Presenting your slide show using the Slide Show tool displays all the slides in your presentation (except hidden ones, unless you opt to show them). Each slide is displayed until you tell the computer to move onto the next slide using your mouse or keyboard – this is called a *Manual Advance*. You can choose to show a specified range of slides if you wish, or you can set up your presentation to run continuously (at an exhibition perhaps).

These options are specified in the Slide Show dialog box.

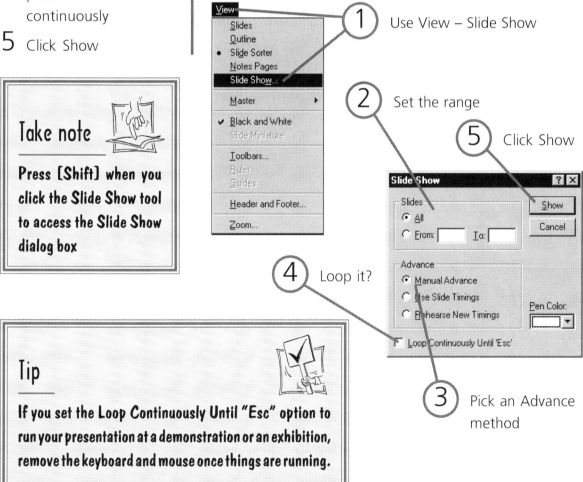

① Use View – Slide Show

② Set the range

⑤ Click Show

④ Loop it?

③ Pick an Advance method

Take note

Press [Shift] when you click the Slide Show tool to access the Slide Show dialog box

Tip

If you set the Loop Continuously Until "Esc" option to run your presentation at a demonstration or an exhibition, remove the keyboard and mouse once things are running.

Summary

- Use the Transition feature to modify the way your slides advance during the presentation

- The Transition speed is usually best set to Fast – this way your audience's attention remains on your presentation and not on your transition method

- Try the Build feature to gradually build up the main points on your slide

- Slides that you may not need can be Hidden, but remain easily accessible should you require them during the presentation

- Practise your presentation with the Rehearse Timings facility to get your pace right

- Slide timings can be set manually from the Transition dialog box or automatically using from Rehearse Timings

- The Slide Show dialog box is used to specify the slides you want to show, and the advance method you want to use (manual or using slide timings)

- Your slide show can be set to loop continuously from the Slide Show dialog box

12 Printing Presentations

Slide format 138

Printing slides 140

Printing notes pages 142

Printing handouts 143

Printing outline view 145

Summary 146

Slide format

You can print your whole presentation in PowerPoint - the slides, speaker's notes pages, audience handouts and the presentation outline.

You can print copies of your slides onto paper or onto overhead transparencies, or you can create slides using a desktop film recorder, or get a bureau to create the slides for you.

The first stage to printing your presentation is to set up the slide format.

1 Choose Slide Setup from the File menu

2 Select the size from the Slides Sized for field

3 Specify the orientation required for the Slides

4 Specify the orientation required for the Notes, Handouts and Outline

5 Click OK

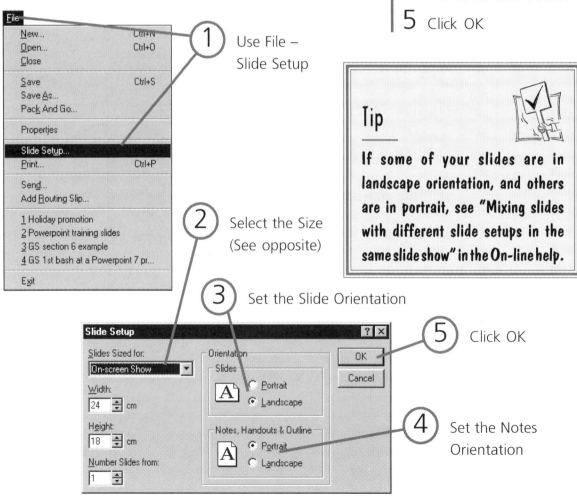

① Use File – Slide Setup

② Select the Size (See opposite)

③ Set the Slide Orientation

④ Set the Notes Orientation

⑤ Click OK

Tip

If some of your slides are in landscape orientation, and others are in portrait, see "Mixing slides with different slide setups in the same slide show" in the On-line help.

Slide Sized for:

Type	Width	Height	Notes
Letter Paper	24 cm	18 cm	3:4 aspect ratio
A4 Paper	26 cm	18 cm	Aspect ratio between that of on-screen show and 35 mm slides
35mm Slides	27 cm	18 cm	Content will fill the slide in landscape orientation 2:3 aspect ratio
Overhead	24 cm	18 cm	Select for overhead transparencies

Printing slides

With the Slide Setup details specified to give the output required, you can go ahead and print your slides.

Basic steps

1 Open the File menu and choose Print

2 Specify the Slide Range to print

3 Set the Number of copies, if required

4 Select one of the Slide options from the Print What: list – see notes opposite

5 Click OK

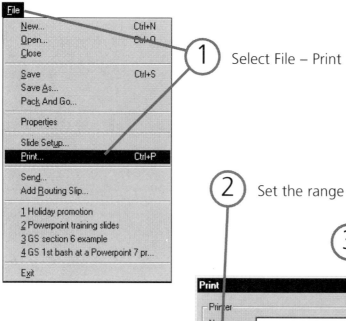

① Select File – Print

② Set the range

③ How many copies?

④ Set the Slide option

⑤ Click OK

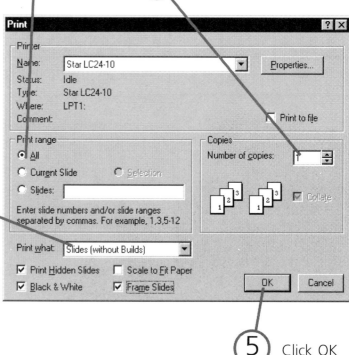

140

Print What: options

Slides

Prints your slides on paper or overhead transparencies, one slide per page. This option is only available when there are no build slides in your presentation.

Slides (with Builds)

Prints each step of a build slide, one image per page, starting with the Slide Title, then each major bullet item in the text.

Slides (without Builds)

Prints one page per build slide, with all items included on it. This option is only available when there are build slides in your presentation.

Tip

You can specify your print range in Slide Sorter view. Select the slides you wish to print from slide sorter view (click on the first one, then shift-click on each additional slide), then in the print range options of the Print dialog box, choose Selection.

Take note

If you are going to send your slides to a service bureau to be turned into 35 mm slides or other materials, choose the Print to File option.

For additional information read the On-line Help or contact the bureau you will be sending the files to.

Printing notes pages

It is useful to print out your notes pages to help ensure you cover all the relevant points during your presentation. When these are printed, a copy of the slide is placed at the top of the page and your notes appear below it.

③ Set the range

② Select Notes Pages

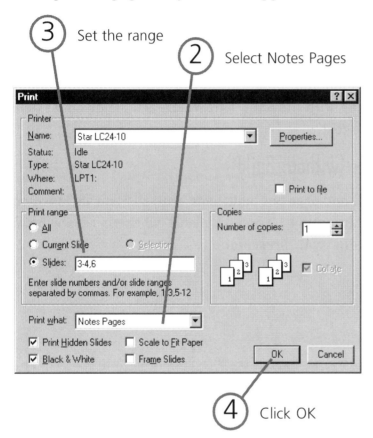

④ Click OK

Take note

If you click the print icon on the standard toolbar, one copy of each slide is printed. For anything else you must access the print dialog box and select what you want to print in the Print What: field.

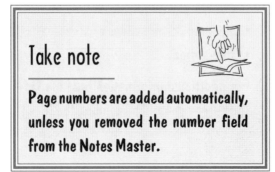

Take note

Page numbers are added automatically, unless you removed the number field from the Notes Master.

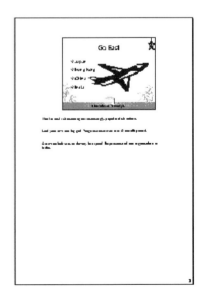

Basic steps

1 Choose Print from the File menu

2 Select Handouts (2 slides, 3 slides or 6 slides per page as required)

3 Specify the Print Range

4 Click OK

Printing handouts

You can print copies of your slides out to issue as audience handouts. The format of the handout can be set up to include 2, 3 or 6 slides to the page.

If you want to add text, ClipArt etc to your handouts, you must edit the Handouts Master page.

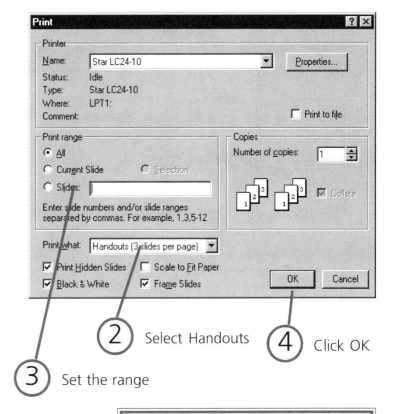

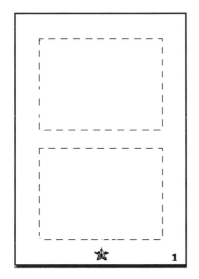

(2) Select Handouts

(4) Click OK

(3) Set the range

Take note

You can print Hidden slides on your handouts, even if you skip them during the presentation.

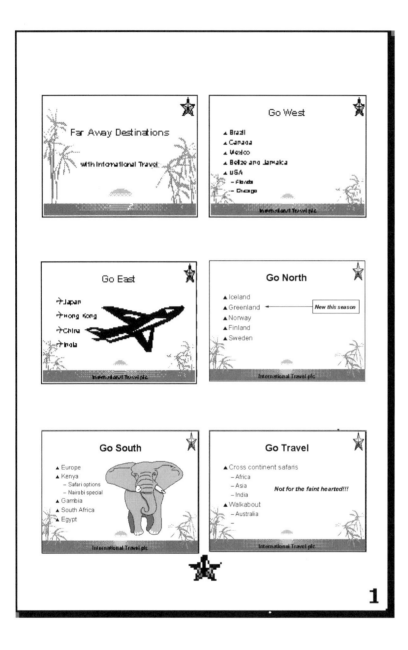

Tip

The 6 slide per page option is a good way to get a summary for your own use. The 3 slide per page option is probably better for your audience as it includes lines down the right side of the page for them to make their own notes.

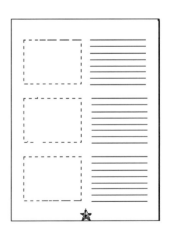

Basic steps

1 Choose Print from the
  File menu
2 Select Outline View
3 Specify the Print Range
4 Click OK

Printing outline view

If you wish to print out a copy of the Outline view of your presentation, the same basic techniques are used. Your print will contain details of each slide title and the main points listed on each slide.

③ Set the Print range

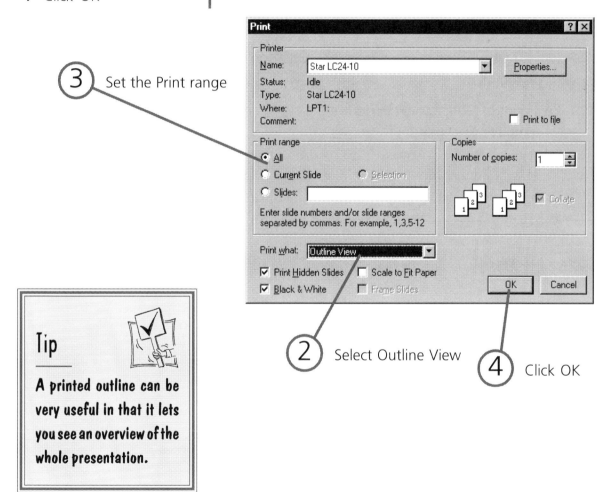

② Select Outline View

④ Click OK

Summary

- Specify your Slide format before printing your presentation

- You can choose to print your slides with or without Builds

- It is often easier to specify your print range (if you don't want to print all of your slides) in slide sorter view

- Print the Notes pages to act as prompts while you give your presentation

- Take a print of Outline view if you want a summary of your complete presentation

Index

A

Adding more items 37
Adding new slides 40
Alignment 46
Animation effects 129
Answer Wizard 16
Arrowheads 77
AutoContent Wizard 4, 34
AutoShapes 75

B

Background styles 52
Blank Presentation 4, 26
Bold 44
Bring Forward 79
Build 128
Bullets 47

C

CD Clips 112
Chart type 88
ClipArt 107
Close Presentation 30
Collapse outline 65

D

Datasheet 86
Delete object 71
Deleting slides 55, 67
Demote 63, 64
Deselect object 70

Drawing tools 73

E

Edit slide text 41
Editing text 61
Exit graph 93
Exit PowerPoint 30
Expand outline 65

F

Fill 76
Flip objects 81, 82
Font 44
Font size 44
Footers 56
Formatting text 44
Free Rotate tool 74

G

Getting into PowerPoint 3
Graphs 84
Gridlines 89
Group objects 80, 82

H

Handouts 2
Headers 56
Help
    Answer Wizard 16
    Contents tab 10
    Find tab 14

Help tool 17
Index tab 13
Slide Show 134
Tip of the Day 3
Tooltip 17
Hide slide 125

I

Increase/decrease paragraph spacing 39
Italics 44

J

Justify 46

K

Keyboard shortcuts 35, 37, 38, 44, 46

L

Layout, changing 48
Legends 89
Line 76
Line styles 77

M

Master
  Handout 119
  Notes 121
  Slide 116
  Title 118
Media clips 110

MIDI Sequencer Clips 111
Move an item 37
Move items 66
Move object 71
Moving through your slides 35

N

New Presentation 28
New slide 62
Notes Pages View 49

O

Objects 6
Open an Existing Presentation 4
Open presentation 31
Organisation chart 96
  Exit 104
  Zoom options 102
Outline 2
Outline view 60

P

PowerPoint dialog box 4
PowerPoint objects 6
PowerPoint window 5
Printing
  Ha

des 140
Promote 63, 64

R

Re-arrange slide order 54
Rehearse Timings 130
Resize object 71
Rotate objects 81, 82

S

Save presentation 29
Select object 70
Selection techniques 36
Send Backward 79
Shadow 76
Slide format 138
Slide layout 48
Slide Navigator 133
Slide notes 49
Slide Show 132

Help 134
Options 135
Slide Sorter view 54, 124
Slide view 48
Slides 2
Sound clips 111
Speaker's Notes 2

T

Tables 105
Template 4, 24, 51
Text box 90
Text Color 45
Text tool 72
Timings, display 131
Timings, Rehearse 130
Tip of the Day 3
Toolbar
Drawing 70
Drawing+ 78
Graph 87
Outlining 60
Transitions 126

U

Underline 44
Ungroup objects 80, 82

V

View/hide datasheet 86
Views 49

W

Wizard, AutoContent 4